THE COUNCILS OF THE CHURCH

THE COUNCILS OF THE CHURCH

A Short History

Norman P. Tanner

A Herder and Herder Book
The Crossroad Publishing Company
New York

The Crossroad Publishing Company
481 Eighth Avenue, New York, NY 10001

Originally published in Italian under the title *I Concili della Chiesa*
© 1999 by Editoriale Jaca Book SpA, Milan

Published in French under the title *Conciles et Synodes*
© 2000 by Les Éditions du Cerf, Paris.

English copyright © 2001 by Norman P. Tanner

Library of Congress Cataloging-in-Publication Data

Tanner, Norman P.
     The councils of the church : a short history / Norman P. Tanner.
          p.   cm.
     "A Herder and Herder book."
     Includes bibliographical references and index.
     ISBN 0-8245-1904-3 (alk. paper)
     1. Councils and synods, Ecumenical—History.   I. Title.
BR200.T36 2001
262'.52—dc21
                                                                    2001000558

1   2   3   4   5   6   7   8   9   10   05   04   03   02   01

Contents

Note and Abbreviations

References to works in the Bibliography are given within square brackets, with the section of the bibliography indicated first. Thus "[2a Chadwick, 1972]" refers to the article by H. Chadwick, published in 1972, in section 2a of the bibliography. References to other works, including those to the abbreviations below, are also given in square brackets.

AAS   *Acta Apostolicae Sedis*

A-T   G. Alberigo and others, ed. *Conciliorum oecumenicorum decreta*, 3d ed. Bologna: Istituto per le scienze religiose, 1973.—N. P. Tanner, *Decrees of the Ecumenical Councils*. London: Sheed & Ward; Washington: Georgetown University Press, 1990. "Tanner" preserves the pagination of "Alberigo," while adding an English translation; hence only one page number is given in references.

D-H   H. Denzinger and P. Hünermann. *Enchiridion symbolorum, definitionum et declarationum de rebus fidei et morum*, 37th ed. Freiburg im Breisgau: Herder, 1991.

Mansi   G. D. Mansi and others, eds. *Sacrorum conciliorum nova et amplissima collectio*, 53 vols. Florence, Venice, Paris, and Leipzig, 1759–1927. Reprinted, Graz: Akademische Druck- und Verlaganstalt, 1960–62, with an index volume.

PG   J. P. Migne, ed. *Patrologia Graeca*, 162 vols. Paris, 1857–66.

PL   J. P. Migne, ed. *Patrologia Latina*, 221 vols. Paris, 1844–64.

Glossary

It is almost impossible to square the circle of correctness and be acceptable politically to all parties concerned, while at the same time using words that are intelligible in their meaning—especially where religion is concerned. Below, therefore, is a brief guide to some words and phrases used in the book, based largely on convention and convenience.

canon—See "decree."

Catholic—Shorter form of "Roman Catholic."

conciliarism—(1) Government by councils. (2) Assertion of the superiority of councils over the pope.

conservatives—"Conservatives/traditionalists" and "liberals/progressives" are terms used principally with regard to Vatican I and II [see pp. 87–88 and 100–101]. The labels, though oversimplifications and far from perfect, are perhaps the best way to indicate two parties or tendencies.

constitution—See "decree."

council—See pp. 2–3.

Counter-Reformation—The Roman Catholic response to the Reformation, ca. 1540–ca. 1650.

decree—(1) General term for any statement promulgated by a council. (2) A particular type of "decree," alongside canon, constitution, creed, declaration, etc. For the usage in Vatican II, see p. 110.

eastern church(es)—In origin the church of the eastern part of the Roman empire: Constantinople was the capital city and became the principal patriarchal see. Largely Greek speaking, hence sometimes called the Greek church. Now includes both the Orthodox Church and other churches of the East.

ecumenical (council)—See p. 3.

Gallicans—Supporters of a French (Gallic) church in communion with Rome but not accepting papal jurisdiction and favoring "conciliarism" (2); prominent from the 15th to the 19th centuries.

Gregorian reform—The reform movement in the late eleventh century, taking its name from Pope Gregory VII (1073–1085).

general (council)—See pp. 46–51.

liberals—See "conservatives."

oriental churches—Churches of the East not in communion with Rome, other than the Orthodox Church.

oriental Catholic churches—Churches of the East in communion with Rome

Orthodox Church—Church(es) acknowledging the primacy of the patriarch of Constantinople.

Protestants—Another word for "Reformers," inasmuch as they protested against the Roman Catholic Church.

Reformation—The sixteenth century reformation in the western church, starting at the time of Martin Luther.

Reformed/Reformers—Pertaining to the "Reformation."

Roman Catholic—Pertaining to the church of Rome, used mainly after the sixteenth-century Reformation.

synod—See pp. 2–3.

Ultramontanes—Supporters of strong papal authority—Rome lying "beyond the (Alps) mountains" (*ultra montes*) from the perspective of northern Europe: very hostile to "conciliarism" (2).

uniate churches—Disliked term for "oriental Catholic churches."

western church—In origin the church of the western part of the
Roman empire: Rome was the capital city and the patriarchal see. Latin speaking, hence often called the Latin
church. Now includes the Roman Catholic Church and the
churches of the Reformation.

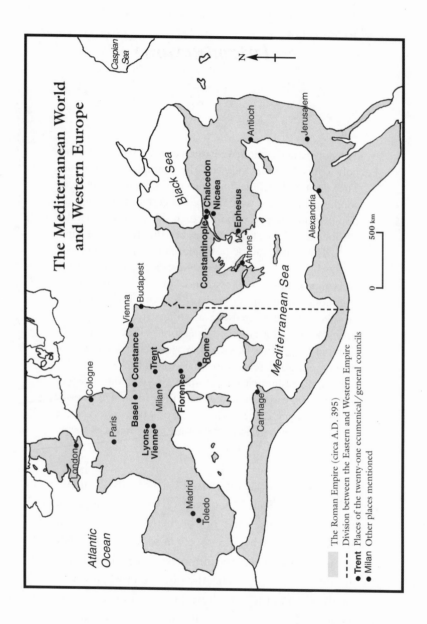

The Mediterranean World and Western Europe

Caspian Sea

Black Sea

Antioch

Jerusalem

Chalcedon
Nicaea
Constantinople
Ephesus
Athens

Alexandria

500 km

0

Budapest

Vienna

Mediterranean Sea

Cologne

Constance

Basel

Trent

Milan

Florence

Rome

Paris

Lyons
Vienne

Carthage

London

Madrid
Toledo

Atlantic Ocean

N

The Roman Empire (circa A.D. 395)

- - - Division between the Eastern and Western Empire

● **Trent** Places of the twenty-one ecumenical/general councils

● Milan Other places mentioned

Introduction

> The holy fathers, who have gathered at intervals in the four holy councils, have followed the examples of antiquity. They dealt with heresies and current problems by debate in common, since it was established as certain that when the disputed question is set out by each side in communal discussions, the light of truth drives out the shadows of lying.
>
> The truth cannot be made clear in any other way when there are debates about questions of faith, since everyone requires the assistance of his neighbour. As Solomon says in his proverbs: "A brother who helps a brother shall be exalted like a strong city; he shall be as strong as a well established kingdom" [Proverbs 18:19]. Again in Ecclesiastes he says: "Two are better than one, for they have a good reward for their toil" [Ecclesiastes 4:9]. And the Lord himself says: "Amen I say to you, if two of you agree on earth about anything they ask, it will be done for them by my Father in heaven. For where two or three are gathered in my name, there am I in the midst of them" [Matthew 18:19]. [A-T, p. 19]

Thus spoke the Christians gathered for the fifth council of the whole church, the Second Council of Constantinople in 553. They began by praising the work of the four previous ecumenical councils, Nicaea I in 325 to Chalcedon in 451, then they reflected more widely on the importance of discussion within the community of the church. Already, therefore, in the middle of the sixth century, the church was aware and proud of its conciliar tradition. Over fourteen centuries later, at the dawn of the church's third millennium, we too can look back and marvel at

1

this tradition which has continued throughout the church's history and produced in our own time one of the most remarkable of all councils, Vatican II. This short book is an exploration of this rich vein in our Christian past.

* * *

The title of the book is *The Councils of the Church*. A few words of explanation about the word *council* and the related term *synod* are in order at the outset. Only recently have council and synod become distinguishable. In the 1960s Pope Paul VI, following the promptings of the Second Vatican Council, introduced into the Roman Catholic Church biennial synods of bishops whose purpose was to advise the pope on certain issues [see below p. 118]. Thus there emerged a distinction between synods, whose role was merely advisory or consultative, and councils, which have legislative or executive powers, such as Vatican II. The distinction was made formal and enshrined in canons 342–48 of the 1983 Code of Canon Law.

The distinction, therefore, is a recent innovation and it applies only to the Roman Catholic Church. Until the 1960s, and therefore throughout almost all the period to be surveyed in this book, the terms *synod* and *council* were virtually synonymous. This is to be expected inasmuch as the two words in English (and similar pairs of words in most European languages: *synode, concile* in French, *sínodo, concilio* in Spanish, *sinodo, concilio* in Italian, *Synode, Konzil* in German), derive from words in Greek and Latin, namely σύνοδος and *concilium* (Latin has also *synodus*, a transliteration of the Greek word), that mean "assembly," without regard to its advisory or executive character. In this book, hereafter, for the sake of convenience, *council* will be the word normally used since it is the more usual English term.

The Greek σύνοδος—we rightly start with Greek since it was the language of the large majority of the early councils—is a compound of two words, σύν meaning "together," and ὁδός meaning "way" or "journey." The sense is that of an assembly of traveling companions, people meeting for a purpose, with a partly unknown future before them, in hope and expectation: a beautiful image of the pilgrim church. Σύνοδος is a feminine noun in Greek; the Latin *synodus* is feminine too, though *concilium* is neuter. So while almost all the participants in the church's major councils were men—not quite all, as we shall see—there was this feminine aspect about the assemblies.

In origin, σύνοδος was a term for any assembly, whether secular or religious. Only later was it restricted largely to church councils. Much the same may be said of the word οἰκουμενική, "ecumenical" in English, and since the ecumenical councils of the church will provide the main focus of this book, this word should also be introduced. It means "inhabited," "where there are houses" (οἶκοι), and by extension "pertaining to the whole (inhabited) world." Hence when applied to councils, it meant assemblies of people from all parts of the Roman Empire—which was regarded by many citizens as coextensive with the inhabited (or civilized) world—as distinct from regional or other local assemblies. Professor Henry Chadwick has shown that the earliest "ecumenical councils" that we know of were not assemblies of churchmen but of actors, athletes, and linen-workers: international trades union congresses, as it were [2a, Chadwick, 1972, pp. 132–35]. Later the Christian church adopted the term for its own assemblies: those that represented the whole church as distinct from regional or provincial councils.

* * *

Regarding the ecumenical councils, four issues have to be confronted. First, which councils are to be regarded as ecumenical? The question is of vital importance because ecumenical councils are generally considered to be of binding authority upon all

Christians, as distinct from local councils, which are binding
upon a locality or for a period of time only. The issue will surface frequently in the book, but the main points are worth mentioning now. The ecumenicity of the first seven councils, from
Nicaea I to Nicaea II in 787, is widely accepted today; though it
was much less clear at the time. The main difficulties arise with
the subsequent councils: Constantinople IV, the ten medieval
councils from Lateran I to Lateran V, which took place after the
schism between the eastern church and the western, and the
three councils after the Reformation, namely Trent, Vatican I,
and Vatican II. Can these later councils be called ecumenical or
are they rather general councils of the western church or, for the
last three, of the Roman Catholic Church?

Second, which documents are to be regarded as the decrees
of a given ecumenical (or general) council? For the last three
councils mentioned above (Trent and Vatican I and Vatican II)
there is little difficulty in deciding since all of them published
their decrees shortly after the conclusion of the council. For the
councils predating the advent of printing, promulgation is less
easily defined. The Council of Ephesus in 431 is the most
famous case. The council broke up without any common agreement among those summoned to it and therefore without any
recognized decrees. Only later, with the reconciliation between
Cyril of Alexandria and John of Antioch, was some measure of
agreement reached; but even then it was unclear which decrees
had met with approval. The Council of Constance (1414–1418)
is another example. Should its resolutions asserting superiority
over the pope be included? Most other cases involve less important matters, and most major decrees, especially the doctrinal
ones, belong unequivocally to a particular council. Although the
importance of the issue should not be exaggerated, it has to be
born in mind.

Third and linked to the second question, what was the
intended authority of a given decree? There is a basic distinction,

recognized even in the early councils, between doctrinal decrees and disciplinary ones. The former concerned matters of doctrine and were intended to have an absolute and timeless quality: at least they couldn't be changed or rejected, even though they might be open to further development and clarification with regard to their expression. Disciplinary decrees, on the other hand, concerned morals and church order: sometimes they were intended to be unalterable and to express divine or natural law, for example, the prohibition against simony, that is, the buying or selling of church offices; at other times less absolute or permanent decrees were intended, for example, those concerning the rubrics of the liturgy or the duties of the clergy. In the case of the Second Vatican Council, the documents were graded as "declarations," "decrees," and "constitutions," in ascending order of authority. In many cases, however, the status of the document has to be surmised and interpreted and it is not stated explicitly; though all of them must be seen within the authoritative framework of ecumenical (or general) councils.

Fourth, establishing the texts of the decrees. In other words, after it has been decided which councils are to be regarded as ecumenical and which decrees are to be regarded as having been promulgated by them, the work remains of establishing the texts of the decrees. Here there is little difficulty with the councils that took place after the advent of printing, since they resulted in the publication of a standard text. For councils predating this period, however, a unique original text normally does not survive: either because the original was lost or because multiple copies were made initially, so that there never was a single original text. For this earlier period, therefore, it is necessary to collate and edit several or many manuscripts and inevitably there are discrepancies among them. Fortunately the discrepancies are, for the most part, slight. This is not surprising because of the importance of the decrees in the church's tradition. Christians have preserved them as carefully and accurately as possible, because people living in a predominantly oral culture tend to have excellent memories, much better than ours today, and partly because many of the texts, notably the creeds, were fairly short or intended for oral recitation. Nevertheless, critical editions of council texts are necessary, and there is plenty of room for better editions.

To put these four issues in context, they are not unique to the councils. Similar problems are faced by biblical scholars and indeed by scholars of other composite works that predate printing. Thus biblical scholars have to decide which books are to be included in the canon of Scripture, which chapters and verses make up a given book, the authority or literary genre of a given book, or part of it, and finally what is the best critical edition of the text. Most people interested in the councils rightly wish to go beyond these textual and critical issues to the ideas contained in the decrees, just as most people are more interested in the theology and spirituality of the Bible than in how it came to be composed. Nevertheless it is important to be aware of the critical and textual issues at the outset: they form part of the framework of any serious study and are waived aside at our peril.

* * *

Appreciating the decrees requires some recognition of the labors of editors who have transmitted them to us. In the early and medieval periods many important texts, such as creeds and disciplinary canons, were preserved with great care; but the decrees of the councils were never collected together, not even those of the ecumenical councils, partly because of the difficulties already mentioned under the four points above, and partly on account of the labor and expense of copying long documents by hand, usually onto parchment. The advent of printing at the end of the Middle Ages dramatically reduced the cost of large works, and the Reformation controversies of the sixteenth century added an incentive to compiling collections of councils. Particularly Roman Catholic scholars, in the wake of the Counter-Reformation, were eager to justify Roman Catholic positions against Reformers by appeal to what the early councils of the church had taught. They were interested, too, in the medieval general councils because they wished to show that these councils were truly ecumenical and therefore could not be rejected in the way that most Reformers wished. The disputes between Gallicans and Ultramontanes [see glossary, p. x] within the Roman Catholic communion as to the authority of councils and the papacy added a further stimulus, inasmuch as both parties sought to justify their positions by appeal to the early and medieval councils. As a result, the great collections of conciliar decrees begin in the early sixteenth century.

The first was the two volumes published in 1524 by the French theologian and canon of Notre Dame cathedral in Paris, Jacques Merlin, *Tomus primus quatuor conciliorum generalium, quadraginta septem conciliorum provincialium* and *Secundus tomus conciliorum generalium.* Soon to follow was *Concilia omnia, tam generalia, quam particularia* (2 vols.; Cologne, 1538), edited by Peter Crabbe, a Belgian Franciscan, which was augmented by a third volume in 1551. Lawrence Surius, a German Carthusian, added a fourth volume, also published in Cologne, in 1567. Using this edition, Domenico Bollani, bishop of Brescia, and D. Nicolini published in Venice in 1587 *Conciliorum omnium tam generalium quam provincialium . . . volumina quinque.*

Scholars in Rome, working under the auspices of Pope Paul V and including the Jesuit Cardinal Robert Bellarmine, produced between 1608 and 1612 the four-volume work, Τῶν ἁγίων οἰκουμενικῶν συνόδων τῆς καθολικῆς ἐκκλησίας ἅπαντα: *Concilia generalia ecclesiae catholicae Pauli V pontificis maximi auctoritate edita*, usually referred to as the "Roman edition" (*Editio Romana*). It sought to be authoritative in deciding which councils were ecumenical or general and which decrees were promulgated by them.

French Jesuits Philip Labbe and Gabriel Cossart, using especially collections by Severin Binius and the *Collectio regia* published in Paris in 1644, published their massive *Sacrosancta concilia* in seventeen volumes in 1671–1672. This was supplemented by an important volume by Stephen Baluze, *Nova collectio conciliorum* (Paris, 1683), and then further expanded into collections by Jean Hardouin and Nicholas Coleti, respectively *Conciliorum collectio regia maxima* (Paris, 1714–1715), and *Sacrosancta concilia* (Venice, 1728–1733).

These labors culminated in the monumental *Sacrorum conciliorum nova et amplissima collectio* in fifty-three volumes, edited by G. D. Mansi and others (Florence, Venice, Paris, and Leipzig, 1759–1927). Giovanni Mansi, a priest of Lucca in Italy and later its archbishop, began his great work as a supplement to Coleti's *Sacrosancta concilia*, mentioned above; and subsequently he and Antonio Zatta published a reissue of both parts as the *Amplissima collectio*, which appeared in thirty-one volumes between 1759 and 1798. The text ends abruptly in the middle of the Council of Florence in the fifteenth century; later councils up to and including Vatican I were covered in the volumes issued by J. B. Martin and L. Petit in the years 1901–1927, taking the series to fifty-three volumes. The whole work was reprinted at Graz in 1960–1962 together with an index volume.

The great strength of "Mansi" (as the collection is known) is its completeness. The scholarship is very imperfect—Mansi rarely corrected proofs and often did not trouble to read the texts he was reprinting, so that there is some confusion and repetition in the documents!—but it is astonishing how many texts are still most readily found in this work. Covering numerous local councils as well as the ecumenical and general ones, it includes the decrees promulgated by the councils and a vast amount of background material, called generically "acts" (Latin *acta*), such as lists of those attending the councils, minutes of meetings, speeches made, and so on. Indeed, Mansi is for councils what Migne's *Patrologia Graeca* and *Patrologia Latina* are for the fathers of the church.

Despite the remarkable scope of the work of Mansi and his collaborators, there remained plenty of further editing to be done. The nineteenth and twentieth centuries saw advances on two fronts in particular: first, more complete collections of the provincial and other local councils of individual countries or regions; second, better editions of the acts and decrees of the ecumenical and general councils. J. Helmrath (1, Helmrath, 1997, cols. 351–55) and Klaus Schatz (1, Schatz, 1997, "Sources") have provided useful brief surveys of these advances.

Of these subsequent editions of the acts of the ecumenical and general councils, especially important are those of the early councils edited by E. Schwartz and others, *Acta Conciliorum Oecumenicorum* (Berlin-Leipzig, 1914–). Twenty-two volumes have been produced so far, reaching the middle of the Second Council of Constantinople in 680–681, well on the way to the final destination envisaged, Nicaea II in 787. For Constance: H. Finke and others, *Acta Concilii Constanciensis*, 4 vols. (Münster, 1896–1928). For Florence: *Concilium Florentinum. Monumenta et Scriptores*, edited by the Pontificio Istituto Orientale, 11 vols. (Rome, 1940–1976). For Trent: *Concilium Tridentinum. Diariorum, Actorum, Epistularum, Tractatuum Nova Collectio*, edited by Societas Gorresiana (Görres-Gesellschaft), 13 vols. so far (Freiburg im Breisgau, 1901–). For Vatican I: *Acta et Decreta Sacrorum Conciliorum Recentiorum. Collectio Lacensis (Coll. Lac.) VII* (Freiburg, 1892). For Vatican II: *Acta et Documenta Concilio Oecumenico Vaticano II Apparando*, series 1 in 4 vols. (16 tomes), for the antepreparatory acts and documents, series 2 in 3 vols. (8 tomes), for the preparatory acts and documents (Vatican City, 1960–1969); *Acta Synodalia Sacrosancti Concilii Oecumenici Vaticani II*, 6 vols. (32 tomes)

so far (Vatican City, 1970–), for the acts of the council itself, also
one volume of indices and two volumes of appendices.

For the decrees of the ecumenical and general councils, the
most important event has been the publication in 1962 of *Conciliorum Oecumenicorum Decreta*, commissioned by *Istituto per
le scienze religiose* in Bologna, Italy, and edited by a team of
scholars led by Professor Giuseppe Alberigo. The work provided
a critical edition of all the decrees of all twenty councils traditionally recognized by the Roman Catholic Church as ecumenical and general councils, from Nicaea I to Vatican I. It was
completed and presented to Pope John XXIII shortly before the
opening of the Second Vatican Council. In a third edition in
1973 the decrees of Vatican II were added and improvements
were made to the texts of various earlier councils. This third edition remains the standard collection of all the ecumenical and
general councils, though further work has been done on a number of individual councils.

I had the privilege of being the general editor, coordinat-
ing a team of twenty-nine translators, of an English version of
Alberigo's edition. *Decrees of the Ecumenical Councils*, published
in 1990 by Sheed and Ward of London and Georgetown University Press of Washington, reproduces photographically the
original Greek and Latin texts of "Alberigo" and provides an
English translation to face each page of the original. In addition,
the notes and introductions of "Alberigo" are translated into
English and the bibliographies are updated, giving some idea of
work accomplished after 1973. In this way the decrees of all the
ecumenical councils are made available to the wider English-
speaking readership who cannot understand readily the ancient
languages. Subsequently an original-Italian edition appeared in
1991, *Conciliorum oecumenicorum decreta: Edizione bilingue*,
edited by G. Alberigo and published by Edizioni Dehoniane of
Bologna, and an original-French edition in 1994, *Les conciles
oecuméniques*, edited by G. Alberigo and published by Éditions

du Cerf of Paris. An original German edition, under the direction of Joseph Wohlmuth, is forthcoming, and a translation into Malayalam is being prepared by Professor Francis Thonippara of Dharmaram College, Bangalore.

Having seen how the councils have come down to us today, it is now time to explore their treasures.

CHAPTER ONE

Ecumenical Councils of the Early Church

List of the Ecumenical Councils

Seven councils are generally recognized as ecumenical by both the eastern and the western church since they took place before the schism of the two churches in the eleventh century: Nicaea I in 325, Constantinople I in 381, Ephesus in 431, Chalcedon in 451, Constantinople II in 553, Constantinople III in 680–681, and Nicaea II in 787. They are often spoken of as the seven councils of the undivided church and hold a privileged place in the Christian tradition.

Why is Nicaea I considered to be the first ecumenical council? What about earlier councils, such as the Council of Jerusalem mentioned in chapter 15 of the Acts of the Apostles? The choice is something of a historical accident. The meeting in Jerusalem, in which "the apostles and elders gathered together" to consider circumcision and other observances of the Jewish law, might indeed be considered a council representing the whole church, and so perhaps could the assembly on Pentecost day or the Last Supper. After the dispersal of the apostles soon after the Council of Jerusalem, however, the possibility of an assembly representing the whole church became remote. Distances and intermittent persecutions made such an assembly—Christians gathering from the four corners of the Roman Empire and beyond—virtually impossible. There were, however, local councils—notably in North Africa and Asia Minor—during this time, showing that the church's conciliar tradition goes right back to the apostolic age and that the guidance of the Holy Spirit working through the community was seen as the most effective way of achieving harmony and resolving difficulties.

What is clear is that by the time the ecumenical councils start to be numbered, principally at the Council of Chalcedon in 451, as we shall see, Nicaea I is listed as the first of them, not the Council of Jerusalem or the gathering on Pentecost day or a later assembly. Perhaps the gap of almost three centuries, from the time of Acts to 325, was just too great for minds to consider an institutional continuity and ancestry. Maybe too it was thought that assemblies of the apostles should not be put into the same category as later gatherings.

The event that made an ecumenical council possible was the peace brought to the church by the conversion to Christianity of the Emperor Constantine. The establishment of Christianity as the favored religion of the Roman Empire meant that bishops could come from a distance and meet without disturbance. Indeed it was Constantine himself who summoned the Council of Nicaea and offered to pay the expenses of travel and accommodation for those who attended. The council did not refer to itself as "ecumenical," but rather as "great" and "sacred" [A-T, pp. 7 and 16; though see p. 12 for "ecumenical" in one MS.]. This is not surprising, however, inasmuch as the word *ecumenical* had not yet become a technical term distinguishing those councils representing the whole church from others of lesser authority. Even in the descriptions of Constantinople I and Ephesus, which came to be counted as the second and third ecumenical councils, although the word *ecumenical* is sometimes used [A-T, pp. 29 and 62–64], it is doubtful whether the word was being used in a technical sense.

The decisive moment in establishing the list of ecumenical councils came at the Council of Chalcedon in 451. This council, in its "definition of faith," repeated the decisions of Nicaea I, Constantinople I, and Ephesus, but no other councils, and referred to itself as "the sacred and great and ecumenical council," thus adding to Nicaea's descriptions of "sacred" and "great" the adjective "ecumenical" [below, pp. 26–29]. *Ecumenical* thus became a technical term and the canon of ecumenical councils was established. Confirmation came with the next three councils, Constantinople II, Constantinople III, and Nicaea II. They repeated Chalcedon's list of ecumenical councils before adding themselves [A-T, pp. 108-13, 124–27, and 133–35].

Participants and Procedures

For considering the members and procedures of the early ecumenical councils, Nicaea I makes a good starting point. Athanasius, who attended the council in his capacity as the deacon and secretary of Bishop Alexander of Alexandria in Egypt, said, toward the end of his life and after giving various other figures, that 318 bishops attended the council [*Synodal Letter to the Bishops of Africa*, dated 368/372, chapter 2]. This became the traditional number, though it is probably a symbolic figure, based on the 318 retainers that Abraham led out to Dan in order to rescue Lot (Genesis 14:14). Scholars today, as well as various writers at the time, have put the likely figure at between 250 and 300. Only a handful of them came from the West: two priests who attended as legates of the bishop of Rome; Bishop Ossius (or Hosius) of Cordoba in Spain, the confidant of Emperor Constantine and an important figure at the council, and at most half a dozen others, so far as we know. Some twenty or so came from North Africa and the Nile valley, a determined group led by the bishop of Alexandria, the most important see in the region. The rest came from the Greek-speaking eastern church, covering present-day Greece and the southern Balkans, Bulgaria, Turkey, Lebanon, Palestine, parts of Jordan and Syria, and the islands of the eastern Mediterranean, notably Crete and Cyprus [1, Dumeige, 1963–, i, pp. 300–301].

The pattern of attendance at the other early councils mostly followed that of Nicaea I. For Constantinople I, the second ecumenical council, a hundred and fifty became the traditionally accepted number of participants, and there is no reason to doubt its approximate accuracy. Probably all the participants came from the eastern church, none from the other two regions, North Africa and the West. At Ephesus the participants came almost exclusively from the eastern and African churches; the West was represented only by two papal legates. At Chalcedon, the largest council of the undivided church, all the five to six hundred participants appear to have been easterners except two papal legates and two bishops from Africa. Easterners also dominated membership of the next three councils, Constantinople II, Constantinople III, and Nicaea II; African participation disappeared from the last two of them as a result of Islam's conquest of North Africa in the seventh century.

The preponderance of eastern participants at the first seven councils is unsurprising inasmuch as they were all held either in or near Constantinople, the eastern capital of the empire. This reminds us that the main driving force behind the early councils was the eastern church. The next most important contribution came from the African church, centered on the see of Alexandria, in terms of both the number of participants and the significance of the debates. Its role was decisive at both Nicaea I and Ephesus, and it set the agenda for several other councils. The contribution of the western church, at least until Chalcedon in 451, was minor. This point is significant because Christianity is often criticized today for being too western, an export of western Europe to the wider world. Yet for the first third of its history the most crucial contributions, at least in terms of councils, came from Asia and Africa. It may be hoped—if a more personal comment may be permitted—that Christians from these two continents, which are such areas of growth for the church today, will become more aware of their early Christian past and recover it for their own traditions, so that Christianity becomes more proper and less alien to them.

Language also underlines the contributions of the East and Africa. Greek was the language both of the eastern church and the church of North Africa under the see of Alexandria, and it dominated as the medium of debate and the language in which all the decrees were promulgated. Latin, the language of the West, including the western part of North Africa, played only a minor role.

The core members of ecumenical councils have always been bishops. This is true for the first seven councils as well, although others took part. When the bishop of Rome sent legates, they were usually priests. Arius, the central figure at Nicaea I, was also a priest, and other clerics below the rank of bishop are known to have attended. Of the laymen, the most prominent were the eastern emperors, who took part in the councils either in person or through officials, who were sometimes numerous. Some women participated. The Empress Pulcheria was the main organizer of the Council of Chalcedon and probably attended its sixth session. Empress Irene was the principal architect of Nicaea II and certainly attended its final session as copresident with her son, the young emperor Constantine VI. Were the laity members of the councils or merely present at them? Recent councils distinguish members with voting rights and others who attend without the right to vote. But in the early councils membership was not so clearly defined, so that participation is usually the better term, and certainly some of the lay people in question were participants.

One reason for the blurred edges of membership was the

principle of unanimous consent. That is to say, in order for a decree to be passed, consent had to be unanimous or at least by an overwhelming majority. Consent was normally by acclamation, expressing the collective mind of those present, rather than by a precise counting of votes. As a result, it was not normally necessary to distinguish clearly between members of the council and others merely in attendance.

The principle of unanimity, or quasi unanimity, was a very important one. It meant that a council could go forward and make binding decisions but in such a way that most people were kept on board, thus minimizing subsequent divisions within the church. Formulas had to be found that were sufficiently elastic as to be acceptable to the minority groups. Thus at Nicaea I a creed was found that in the end was acceptable to all but two bishops and the priest Arius; Ephesus was deadlocked precisely because unanimity could not be achieved; Chalcedon and the later councils took time and trouble to find formulas that were widely acceptable to the participants. As a result, part of the genius of the ecumenical councils was their contribution to keeping the church largely united during its first millennium.

This principle has been maintained down to today. It is why it was considered important at Trent and Vatican I and Vatican II that consent to the decrees should be as unanimous as possible. This may have much to teach us regarding other aspects of church governance. People expressed themselves strongly both inside and outside the councils and expected others to do likewise. Debate, often fierce, continued after a council, and the need for "reception" of its teachings was acknowledged. Somehow, nevertheless, there was an expectation that common agreement could eventually be reached as well as the willingness to work for it.

Some sense of the successful protocol of the early councils comes—somewhat tongue in cheek—from canon 1 of the Eleventh Council of Toledo in Spain, a provincial council held in 675, which became a classic text and was quoted later by the Councils of Constance and Trent:

> Nobody should shout at or in any way disturb the Lord's priests when they sit in the place of blessing. Nobody should cause disturbance by telling idle stories or jokes or, what is even worse, by stubborn disputes. As the apostle says, "If anyone thinks himself religious and does not bridle his tongue but deceives his heart, then his religion is vain" [James 1:26]. For justice loses its reverence when the silence of the court is disturbed by a crowd of turbulent people. As the prophet says, "the reverence due to justice shall be silence" [Isaiah 32:17]. Therefore, whatever is being debated by the participants, or is being proposed by persons making an accusation, should be stated in quiet tones so that the hearers' senses are not disturbed by contentious voices and they do not weaken the authority of the court by their tumult. Whoever thinks that the aforesaid things should not be observed while the council is meeting, and disturbs it with noise or dissensions or jests, contrary to the things forbidden here, shall leave the assembly, dishonourably stripped of the right to attend, according to the precept of divine law whereby it is commanded, "Drive out the scoffer, and strife will go out with him" [Proverbs 22:10], and he shall be under sentence of excommunication for three days. [Mansi, xi, p. 137; A-T, pp. 406 and 661]

The presence of the eastern emperors at the councils has already been noted. But they were much more than just present. They summoned, presided over, either in person or through their officials, and subsequently promulgated the decrees of all the first seven ecumenical councils. Occasionally the western emperor was also represented, but he never appeared in person and his representation was largely nominal. According to present Roman Catholic canon law, the pope (the bishop of Rome) alone has the right to convene, preside over (in person or through deputies), and to approve the decrees of an ecumenical council [*Codex Iuris Canonici*, 1983, canons 337–41 and 749]. But this must be seen as a regulation that could be changed or modified, since it was not observed during the first half of the church's history.

The question remains whether approval by the bishop of Rome was regarded as necessary. On the one hand, his explicit approval was not invariably expected or even sought, at least immediately. The very important creed of Constantinople I, for example, appears to have received no formal papal approval until after it was accepted by the Council of Chalcedon seventy years later in 451. Popes opposed the summoning of Chalcedon and took time before approving Constantinople II and Nicaea II. On the other hand, the approval of the bishop of Rome was sought as early as Nicaea I, and his sanction gradually came to be accepted as necessary for the decrees of an ecumenical council. But the approval of the other major sees, particularly Constantinople, Alexandria, and Antioch, was also regarded as necessary, so that Rome's consent must be seen within the context of the principle of unanimity, mentioned earlier, rather than as some isolated fiat.

In terms of procedures, therefore, there was both flexibility and continuity. Two extremes of interpretation must be avoided. On the one hand, it is foolish to read back present structures too simply into the early councils, as if everything led inevitably to the present arrangements or, even more naively, as if the present structures were already fully in place then. On the other hand, the councils were aware of their own established principles and protocols, so that it would be wrong to suggest that everything was arbitrary or open-ended. The first seven ecumenical councils form an exceptionally successful strand in the church's history—indeed they are remarkable in world history—and participants at them were aware of their importance. Their significance lies, above all, in the decrees they produced and it is to them that we may now turn.

Doctrinal Decrees:
Nicaea I to Chalcedon

The three most important decrees of the first four ecumenical councils are the creeds of Nicaea I and Constantinople I and the "definition" of Chalcedon. Today we take their contents almost for granted. The creed of Constantinople I, which is a development of the creed of Nicaea I, remains today, almost word for word, the basic creed of most Christian churches and is widely used in the liturgy. The definition of Chalcedon has remained a cornerstone for subsequent developments in theology. These three documents constitute perhaps the most influential statements of Christian belief outside Scripture. Yet our familiarity with them can remove their wonder.

The creed of Nicaea emerged from the controversy that centered around the teachings of Arius (336), who was a popular preacher and parish priest in the city of Alexandria, regarding the divinity of the Son of God, the second person of the Trinity. This creed was accepted by the members of the council as the best formulation of their beliefs, and it condemned the weakened notion of divinity attributed to the Son of God by Arius, though he is not mentioned by name. Precisely how it came to be adopted is unclear from the scanty records of the council. It appears to be based on the confession of faith used in the rite of Baptism by a particular local church—Jerusalem or somewhere in Syria or Palestine is thought by some scholars to be the most likely provenance [2a, Kelly, 1972, pp. 205–30]—to which various anti-Arian words and clauses were added, including the word ὁμοούσιος, translated as "consubstantial" or "of the same being," to describe the Son's relationship with the Father. It may be described as a baptismal creed adapted to provide a conciliar test of orthodoxy. The text is as follows, with the likely added anti-Arian clauses italicized.

> We believe in one God the Father all powerful, maker of all things both seen and unseen. And in one Lord Jesus Christ, the Son of God, the only-begotten begotten from the Father, *that is from the substance of the Father,* God from God, light from light, *true God from true God, begotten not made, consubstantial with the Father,* through whom all things came to be, both those in heaven and those in earth; for us humans and for our salvation he came down and became incarnate, became human, suffered and rose up on the third day, went up into the heavens, is coming to judge the living and the dead. And in the Holy Spirit.
>
> *And those who say "there once was when he was not," and "before he was begotten he was not," and that he came to be from things that were not, or from another hypostasis or substance, affirming that the Son of God is subject to change or alteration—these the catholic and apostolic church anathematises.* [A-T, p. 5]

What is clear from the creed is the amazing creativity, combined with faithfulness to Scripture, of the church in its first three centuries. Prefigurings of the Trinity may be seen already in the Old Testament and much clearer indications in the New, notably in the accounts of the Annunciation (Luke 1:26-38), Christ's baptism (Matthew 3:13-17; Mark 1:9-11; Luke 3:21-22; John 1:29-34) and his discourse at the Last Supper (John 13:31–17:26), in the commission to the disciples to baptize "in the name of the Father and of the Son and of the Holy Spirit" (Matthew 28:19), and in Paul's greeting "The grace of the Lord Jesus Christ and the love of God and the fellowship of the Holy Spirit be with you all" (2 Corinthians 13:13). These, however, fall well short of, or at least differ in style from, the rounded formulation of the relationship between the three persons of the

Trinity, especially regarding their equality and full divinity, that is to be found first in the creed of Nicaea and later and more completely in that of Constantinople I. The apparent simplicity of the creed of Nicaea belies the work that went into producing it. A brilliant miniature, it distills the reflections and prayers of the early church.

The creed of Nicaea proved its worth for more than a century, though the Arian controversy was slow in resolution. The Council of Ephesus in 431 forbade any changes to be made to it, under pain of anathema [*A-T*, p. 65]. At the Council of Chalcedon in 451, however, a deadlock was reached. Many members of the council were unwilling to go beyond the creed of Nicaea, especially in view of Ephesus's prohibitions of change to it. On the other hand, the creed of Nicaea did not seem adequate to the new situation, especially in view of various controversies that had arisen since 325, so that something more needed to be said. It was at this point, we are told, that the archdeacon of Constantinople suggested as a way forward the creed that had been proclaimed by a council held in his city in 381 and that appears to have lain unnoticed by the wider church since then. The Council of Chalcedon proceeded to adopt the creed of 381, claiming it was really one and the same as the creed of 325—by which a legitimate development might be understood—in order not to run foul of the Ephesus prohibition.

We can appreciate why the creed of 381 was seen as an improvement on that of 325. The text is as follows: omissions from the creed of 325 are indicated by insertion marks (^), additions to it are italicized.

> We believe in one God the Father all powerful, maker *of heaven and of earth, and* of all things both seen and unseen. And in one Lord Jesus Christ, the only-begotten Son of God, begotten from the Father *before all the ages,* ^ light from light, true God from true God, begotten not made, consubstantial with the Father, through whom all things

came to be ^ ; for us humans and for our salvation he came down *from the heavens* and became incarnate *from the holy Spirit and the virgin Mary,* became human *and was crucified on our behalf under Pontius Pilate;* he suffered *and was buried* and rose up on the third day *in accordance with the scriptures;* he is coming *again with glory* to judge the living and the dead; *his kingdom will have no end.* And in the Spirit, *the holy, the lordly and life-giving one, proceeding forth from the Father, co-worshipped and co-glorified with Father and Son, the one who spoke through the prophets; in one, holy, catholic and apostolic church. We confess one baptism for the forgiving of sins. We look forward to a resurrection of the dead and life in the age to come. Amen.* ^ . [A-T, p. 24]

The most obvious omission is the concluding paragraph of anti-Arian anathemas. The Arian debate had largely died down by the time of Chalcedon, so that the added paragraph would no longer appear necessary and anyway it was clumsy when recited aloud—recitation at the sacraments of Baptism and the Eucharist being important uses of the creed. The same considerations may explain the omission of the phrase "that is from the substance of the Father" and, regarding the creation of heaven and earth, the Father's role is preferred to the Son's. The additions are more numerous. Besides the Father's role in the creation of heaven and earth, there is a much fuller treatment of the Spirit, reflecting the controversies about the Spirit in the years preceding Constantinople I; there is a concluding section about the church and our salvation; and the life of Christ is filled out. Altogether the style is better for recitation in public, and the contents are more devotional, that is, better suited to popular religion. The skeleton text of 325 has now been fleshed out without sacrificing any of its theological rigor.

The creed of 381 is usually called, in common parlance, the Nicene creed, and in a sense that is correct since it was considered a development of the creed of 325, not something different from it. In scholarly circles, however, it is more accurately called the Nicene-Constantinopolitan creed (often abbreviated to N-C) and that of 325 is called the creed of Nicaea (abbreviated to N), in order to distinguish the two. The creed of 381 has remained until today, with one significant exception, the most important creed of most Christian churches: a remarkable tribute to the early councils.

The exception is the addition of the "Filioque" clause. That is to say, to the words "And in the Spirit . . . proceeding forth from the Father" the western church later added "and the Son" (Latin, *Filioque*), so that the Spirit proceeds from the Son as well as from the Father. The clause was first interpolated into the creed at the Third Council of Toledo in Spain in 589, it spread rapidly within the Frankish empire from the late eighth century onward, partly to combat residual Arianism there by emphasizing the Son's divinity and equality with the Father. The papacy, though initially opposed to the addition, came round to favoring it. The addition was strongly resisted by the eastern church, notably while Photius was patriarch of Constantinople during the late ninth century, both on theological grounds and because it breached the Council of Ephesus's prohibition against changes to the creed. It was a main cause of the schism between the two churches in the eleventh century and has remained a major obstacle to reunion ever since.

This is not the place to enter the controversy further. Our overwhelming sympathies may well be with the eastern church, as mine certainly are, and there seems no real difficulty for the western church simply to remove the clause from the creed, as the Roman Catholic Church has done on a number of occasions recently. Perhaps the greatest moral is the danger of abandoning conciliar government in the church. It was precisely the action of the western church in making the addition without the agreement of an ecumenical council that was wholly unacceptable to the East. The position of the eastern church, however, is not entirely consistent. Ephesus's prohibition against changes referred to the creed of 325—the creed of 381 remained largely unknown until the Council of Chalcedon in 451 and therefore at the time of the Council of Ephesus in 431—so the creed of 381, which the eastern church accepts, is itself in breach of Ephesus's prohibition! It might also be argued that a prohibition against change could not, and was never intended to, prohibit all changes for ever but only those that were unsuitable. Still, the point remains that an addition made to the creed by the West unilaterally, without the consent of the eastern church, must be regarded as unjustifiable.

Recently there was question of a second exception. The liturgical changes after Vatican II brought a change in the opening words of the creed as it was then recited, from the prevailing "I believe" to "We believe." The change caused much discussion and considerable hostility: many people, especially in the English-speaking world, thought that it was symptomatic of the soft and over-communitarian approach of Vatican II. In fact, of course, it was not a deviation from the Nicene creed but rather a return to the original.

The definition of the Council of Chalcedon, the third decree to be examined, is worth looking at in some detail both on account of its theological importance and because it brings together the work of the first four ecumenical councils and makes concrete many points made so far in this book. It reads as follows:

> The sacred and great and ecumenical synod by God's grace and by decree of your most religious and Christ-loving emperors Valentinian Augustus and Marcian Augustus, assembled in Chalcedon, metropolis of the province of Bithynia, in the shrine of the saintly and triumphant martyr Euphemia, issues the following decrees.
>
> In establishing his disciples in the knowledge of the faith, our lord and saviour Christ said: "My peace I give you, my

peace I leave to you," so that no one should disagree with his neighbour regarding religious doctrines but that the proclamation of the truth would be uniformly presented. But the evil one never stops trying to smother the seeds of religion with his own tares and is for ever inventing some novelty or other against the truth; so the Master, exercising his usual care for the human race, roused this religious and most faithful emperor to zealous action and summoned to himself the leaders of the priesthood from everywhere, so that through the working of the grace of Christ, the master of all of us, every injurious falsehood might be staved off from the sheep of Christ and that they might be fattened on fresh growths of the truth.

This is in fact what we have done. We have driven off erroneous doctrines by our collective resolution and we have renewed the unerring creed of the fathers. We have proclaimed to all the creed of the 318; and we have made our own those fathers who accepted this agreed statement of religion, the 150 who later met in great Constantinople and themselves set their seal to the same creed.

Therefore, whilst we also stand by the decisions and all the formulas relating to the creed from the sacred synod which took place formerly at Ephesus, whose leaders of most holy memory were Celestine of Rome and Cyril of Alexandria, we decree that pre-eminence belongs to the exposition of the right and spotless creed of the 318 saintly and blessed fathers who were assembled at Nicaea when Constantine of pious memory was emperor; and that those decrees also remain in force which were issued in Constantinople by the 150 holy fathers in order to destroy the heresies then rife and to confirm this same catholic and apostolic creed.

The creed of the 318 fathers . . . [the creed of Nicaea follows].

And the same of the 150 saintly fathers assembled in Constantinople . . . [the creed of Constantinople follows].

This wise and saving creed, the gift of divine grace, was sufficient for a perfect understanding and establishment of religion. For its teaching about the Father and the Son and the holy Spirit is complete, and it sets out the Lord's becoming human to those who faithfully accept it. . . .

[The synod] has suitably added, against false believers and for the establishment of orthodox doctrines, the letter of the primate of greatest and older Rome, the most blessed and most saintly archbishop Leo, written to the sainted archbishop Flavian to put down Eutyches's evil-mindedness, because it is in agreement with great Peter's confession and represents a support we have in common.

It is opposed to those who attempt to tear apart the mystery of the economy into a duality of sons; and it expels from the assembly of the priests those who dare to say that the divinity of the Only-begotten is passible; and it stands opposed to those who imagine a mixture or confusion between the two natures of Christ; and it expels those who have the mad idea that the servant-form he took from us is of a heavenly or some other kind of being; and it anathematises those who concoct two natures of the Lord before the union but imagine a single one after the union.

So, following the saintly fathers, we all with one voice teach the confession of one and the same Son, our Lord Jesus Christ: the same perfect in divinity and perfect in humanity, the same truly God and truly man, of a rational soul and a body; consubstantial with the Father as regards his divinity, and the same consubstantial with us as regards his humanity; like us in all respects except for sin; begotten before the ages from the Father as regards his divinity, and in the last days the same for us and for our salvation from Mary, the virgin God-bearer, as regards his humanity; one and the same Christ, Son, Lord, only begotten, acknowledged in two natures which undergo no confusion, no change, no division, no separation; at no point was the difference between the natures taken away through the union, but rather the property of both natures is preserved and comes together into a single person and a single subsistent being; he is not parted or divided into two persons, but is one and the same only-begotten Son, God, Word, Lord Jesus Christ, just as the prophets taught from the beginning about him, and as the Lord Jesus Christ himself instructed us, and as the creed of the fathers handed it down to us.

Since we have formulated these things with all possible accuracy and attention, the sacred and ecumenical synod decreed that no one is permitted to produce or even to write down or compose any other creed or to think or teach otherwise. As for those who dare either to compose another creed or even to promulgate or teach or hand down another creed for those who wish to convert to a recognition of the truth from Hellenism or from Judaism, or from any kind of heresy at all: if they be bishops or clerics, the bishops are to be deposed from the episcopacy and the clerics from the clergy; if they be monks or layfolk, they are to be anathematised. [A-T, pp. 83-7]

"The sacred and great and ecumenical synod," the definition begins. "Ecumenical" becomes a technical term. "By God's grace," the council asserts the divine initiative; "and by decree of your most religious and Christ-loving emperors Valentinian Augustus and Marcian Augustus," emphasizes the role of the emperors, although Empress Pulcheria as the chief organizer of the council might well have been included alongside her husband Marcian. In the second paragraph the council roots itself in Christ and in Scripture, aware of the frequent accusation brought against the early councils that they were replacing the Bible with human inventions and philosophical concepts. The paragraph ends with a beautiful image of faithfulness to tradition and proper development, "so that . . . they might be fattened on fresh growths of the truth," growths that are fresh, but of the truth rather than deviations from it.

The decree proceeds in defense of orthodoxy, "We have driven off erroneous doctrines," but immediately it makes a breakthrough, adding to the creed of Nicaea I that of Constantinople I, skillfully getting round Ephesus's prohibition against changes to Nicaea by describing the 381 creed as its "seal." The early councils, notably including Chalcedon, sought to be faithful to the past while confronting the intellectual and other challenges of their day, both within and outside the Christian community: there was little ducking of issues. Further and very importantly—though this is something that is difficult to put one's finger on—the council fathers had an eye for the future: they reached formulations that sensed future developments. The endurance of the creed of 381 and the definition of Chalcedon are outstanding examples of this prescience.

In the fourth paragraph, the Council of Ephesus of 431, which concerned itself chiefly with Mary's title of "mother of God," was approved and thus found its way into the canon as the third ecumenical council. Approval was a bold move inasmuch as it meant both recognition of this turbulent council and rejection of the equally difficult Second Council of Ephesus—called *Latrocinium* or the "Robber Council" by the pope of the time, Leo I—which assembled in 449 and sought to reverse the decisions of the earlier (First) Council of Ephesus. The desire for unanimity is shown in the description of the bishops of Rome and Alexandria, Celestine, and Cyril, as the "leaders" of the council of 431; it was important to bring the churches of the West and of Africa fully into the decisions of an ecumenical council.

Thereafter the decree seems to backtrack, returning twice (the first passage is printed, the second is omitted) to the creeds of Nicaea and Constantinople and the decisions of Ephesus, yet with some clarifications and expansions. The process is indicative of the mood of the early councils: frequent visits to the sources, from which new insights are drawn, cautious steps forward—a desire for consensus all the way.

Finally, the council addresses the specific issue for which it had been summoned, the teaching of Eutyches about the relationship between divinity and humanity in Jesus Christ. Eutyches, a monk of Constantinople, held that, after the incarnation, the one person or hypostasis of the God-man, Jesus Christ, Son of God and son of Mary, was matched by a single nature (Greek, μόνη φύσις, hence monophysite), which included both the divine and the human. The council, making use of the theology contained in the letter, or tome, written shortly before by Pope Leo to Flavian, patriarch of Constantinople, rejected Eutyches's monophysitism and succinctly propounded its own solution of one person in two natures. The decree ends with anathemas against those who dare to compose anything different, but the prohibition did not mean the end of discussion and any new formulations, rather that subsequent developments should be within the framework laid down by the decree. Indeed, Chalcedon's acceptance of the creed of 381, which went beyond that of 325, seems to have been crucial in justifying Chalcedon's own additional formulations and in legitimizing the possibility of further developments in the future.

A few words are in order about language here. Human language, especially about the divine, is always very imperfect, so that the credal formulas of councils must be seen as boundary fences marking danger areas and as signposts to the future, as much as inadequate descriptions. The first two councils, Nicaea I and Constantinople I, were concerned with language about the Trinity; Ephesus and Chalcedon moved on to Christology, the relationship between divinity and humanity in Christ. How could Greek—the dominant language of the eastern empire and already complicated from the Christian point of view by being the medium of the sophisticated philosophy of Plato and Aristotle—be harnessed to express the relatively new concepts of Christian theology? Some idea of the difficulties facing the early councils may be gained from looking up in a dictionary of classical Greek the three words that were eventually accepted as keys: οὐσία for being, as in the one being of God; ὑπόστασις for person, as in the three persons of the Trinity; and φύσις for nature, as in the two natures, human and divine, of Christ. All three words, as the dictionary shows, could express a wide range of different ideas and concepts. For example, ὑπόστασις in classical Greek had the meanings of support, resistance, lying in ambush, jelly or thick soup, sediment in liquids, origin, foundation, substructure, confidence, courage, resolution, steadfastness, promise, substance, reality or nature, wealth or property, and various other things! There was also considerable overlap in the meanings of the three words. To some extent the debates of the early church were exercises in linguistic analysis.

Latin, the second main language of the church of the early councils, the language of the western church, including the western half of North Africa, acted as a handmaid, providing clarifications and sometimes even suggesting words from outside the Greek perspective. Notably, the choice of the word ὁμο-ούσιος (consubstantial), which was a key word in the creed of 325 [above, p. 21] and was retained in that of 381, was almost certainly helped by the fact that similar terms in Latin had been accepted by western theologians for some time before the Council of Nicaea: *unius substantiae* since the time of Tertullian over a century earlier and *consubstantialis* some time later, while ὁμο-ούσιος was of doubtful orthodoxy in eastern theology until its adoption by the Council of Nicaea. Other Latin words, such as *persona* and *natura*, also had an influence.

Just as the vocabulary of Christian theology had to be forged and was not simply a given from the start, so more generally orthodoxy itself was forged by the councils. Christians regarded orthodoxy as being present from the beginning of the Christian era inasmuch as the fullness of revelation was contained in the person and gospel of Jesus Christ. In this sense the task of councils was to defend orthodoxy, and often they spoke fiercely in terms of such defense. But it was not simply a matter of warding off heresy from the citadel of orthodoxy, as if heresies were clearly recognizable from the outset. The expression of orthodoxy, and its articulation in different cultural milieux, had to be worked at and came at the end of a process. Indeed, those who came to be designated as heretics, such as Arius or Nestorius or Eutyches, contributed to the process: without them the debate and the resulting articulation of orthodoxy would not have taken place. The genius of the first four councils was to weave from these various strands—principally regarding the two central mysteries of the Trinity and Jesus Christ—a pattern that has endured and remained fresh to this day.

Doctrinal Decrees:
Constantinople II to Nicaea II

The remaining three ecumenical councils will not detain us long. They are important but less so than the first four councils, so that regrettably in this short book they must be passed over rather quickly. The first two of them, Constantinople II and Constantinople III in 553 and 680–681, may be seen as rounding off the work of the first four councils, especially Chalcedon; Nicaea II in 787 turned to the topic of iconoclasm.

Constantinople II is a rather sad council. Its single decree, the "Three Chapters," which condemns various writings of three earlier supporters of Nestorius—namely, Theodore of Mopsuestia, Theodoret of Cyrrhus, and Ibas of Edessa—resulted from the desire of Emperor Justinian to placate the Egyptian church, which had never reconciled itself to the Council of Chalcedon. The kernel of the decree had been published as an edict of Justinian in 543/544 and a decade later, at Justinian's insistence, it was adopted by the Second Council of Constantinople. There was much unease at condemning three men who had been dead for a century or more and particularly because none of them had been condemned by the Council of Chalcedon; indeed, one letter of Ibas had been explicitly vindicated at Chalcedon. Vigilius, the bishop of Rome, approved the decree only reluctantly. It did not, moreover, have the desired effect with the Egyptian church, where the drift into monophysitism continued. Ironically the finest statement of all the councils on the need for open discussion, quoted at the beginning of this book [above p. 1], comes from this pressurized council!

By the time of the next council, Constantinople III in 680–681, the Arab conquest of North Africa was almost complete. As a result the African contribution to ecumenical councils virtually ceased: one of the greatest disasters for the church in its entire history. While Constantinople II sought to placate the monophysite inclinations of the Egyptian church, Constantinople III tended in the opposite direction by asserting a duality of wills and "principles of action" in Christ, one for his divine nature and another for his human nature, rather than a single one in accordance with his one person or substance. "Each nature wills and performs the things that are proper to it in a communion with the other," the decree concludes succinctly [A-T, p. 129]. The teaching was, of course, not just a matter of speculative theology but exercised a profound effect upon the devotional life of Christians down through the centuries: it ensures that the humanity of Christ is taken seriously—surely a very modern concern—and is not subsumed into his divinity.

One of those condemned by the council for holding monothelite (one will) beliefs was Pope Honorius, who was bishop of Rome from 625 to 638 and who had propounded his unorthodox views in two letters to Sergius, patriarch of Constantinople. The condemnation of him by name was repeated at the next ecumenical council, Nicaea II, and it emerged as a *cause célèbre* when papal infallibility came to be debated at the First Vatican Council of 1869–1870 [A-T, pp. 125 and 135 for the two condemnations]. The authenticity of the two letters is now generally accepted, but there remains the question of the level of authority intended for the views expressed in the two letters and hence the gravity of the pope's error. Regarding their authority, the truth seems to lie somewhere between two extremes. The letters were personal letters from the pope to the patriarch of Constantinople expressing the pope's personal opinions and were not intended to be solemn statements of defined doctrine: on the other hand, any correspondence of this kind is at least semi-official and of some authority, so that the doctrinal error cannot be simply brushed aside as inconsequential. It helps to put the teaching of infallibility into context: this cannot mean freedom from error in all details. The case, however, is an exceptional one and its rarity highlights the remarkable consistency with which the see of Rome came out on the right side—often after much soul-searching—in the doctrinal disputes of the early church: far more consistently than the bishops of other patriarchal sees.

Rather different was the main topic of Nicaea II, the last generally recognized ecumenical council of the undivided church, which was held a century later, in 787. It was images. What kind of reverence, if any, should be paid to images associated with Christ, such as the crucifix, and those of the saints? This topic, too, as well as raising important theological issues, had huge implications for the devotional life of Christians. The debate had been raging, often fiercely and sometimes violently, since the early eighth century, mainly in the Byzantine world. On the one hand, in support of the iconoclasts (those opposed to images) was the Old Testament prohibition against making images (e.g., Exodus 20:4 and Deuteronomy 5:8); the desire to make converts among Jews and Muslims, who abided by the prohibition; monophysitism, which tended to downplay the humanity of Christ and therefore the worth of images of him; dualist tendencies among Manichees, Paulicians, and others, who regarded all matter—including, therefore, images and the human body—as evil; and the influence of neo-Platonic philosophy, which followed Plato in regarding images as but dim reflections of reality. On the other hand, there had been a tradition since the early church of representing Christ and the saints in various forms of imagery. The council both supported the use of images and indicated the type of reverence that could be paid to them, distinguishing between worship (λατρεία), which could be given only to the divine and in no way to images, and veneration or reverence (προσκύνησις), which should be paid to an image on account of the person(s) it represented.

Secular and ecclesiastical politics entered into the iconoclast controversy intimately. That is to say, the imperial family and the Byzantine court divided into iconoclast and iconophile factions along political lines as well as on religious grounds. The single most important figure was the regent Irene, illustrating again the role of women in the councils. Widow of the previous emperor, Leo IV (775–780), and regent for her infant son, she summoned the council, obtained papal support for it, outwitted those who sought to disrupt it, and brought it to a successful conclusion, presiding in person at the final session and ordering the promulgation of the decrees. To temper admiration for her, it might be mentioned that this strong woman later fell out with her son and had him blinded, a traditional punishment in Byzantine court circles. Reception of the council was slow in both East and West and only in the following century was there general acceptance of its decisions.

Canons Relating to Church Order

The councils of the early church are best known for their doctrinal statements. In addition there are the canons relating to church order, sometimes called disciplinary decrees. Four of the seven councils in question issued a series of canons of this kind: Nicaea I, Constantinople I, Chalcedon, and Nicaea II. There are also the canons of the Council of Trullo in 692, which will be discussed in the next section and were regarded as the disciplinary part of the Second and Third Councils of Constantinople.

A brief look at the twenty canons of Nicaea I [A-T, pp. 6–

16], which form the most complete collection of these councils apart from that of Trullo, gives an idea of the remarkable scope and good sense of the early church's concern for proper order. They dispel any notion that the early church lived in an ivory tower of theology divorced from the realities of life.

Thus, the sublime creed of Nicaea, about which we have spoken, is followed immediately by the first canon, "Concerning those who make themselves eunuchs." Men who have undergone castration are prohibited from becoming or remaining clergy, unless the mutilation was done against their will or on medical grounds. The most famous rumored case of such self-mutilation, which the canon may well have had in mind, was that of Origen, the great theologian from Alexandria, a century earlier. The canon thus demands respect for God's creation, including our bodies: a recurrent theme of the councils and an antidote to the dualist tendencies within us.

The second canon warns against promoting men to be priests or bishops too soon after Baptism: "Not a recent convert, or he may be puffed up and fall into the condemnation and snare of the devil" (1 Timothy 3:6-7), quotes the canon. Later in the same century, in 373/374, Ambrose was proclaimed bishop of Milan while he was still a catechumen and was ordained immediately after his Baptism, in evident breach of the canon; likewise in 381 Nectarius was selected by the Emperor Theodosius to be bishop of Constantinople before he had been baptized, and he was ordained bishop straight after his Baptism. So it is important to ponder the authority of the disciplinary canons of the early councils. Many of them were not observed to the letter and were probably never intended to be. Evidently their status varied. The prohibition against self-castration in canon 1 was surely regarded as an absolute, though even in this case the prohibition against ordination may have been open to dispensation. Other canons, including canon 2, were regarded more obviously, or soon became so, as ideals and regulations to be understood and inter-

preted within existing practices and therefore open to exceptions. Where the balance lay is a delicate issue, and so it must
have been for contemporaries too.

Canon 3 concerns women living with the clergy. "This
great synod absolutely forbids a bishop, presbyter, deacon or any
of the clergy to keep a woman who has been brought in to live
with him, with the exception of course of his mother or sister or
aunt or of any person who is above suspicion." If married clergy
were still taken for granted, the context seems to be young
women who lived in the houses of clergy in some form of disci-
pleship. A well-known case in point had been Paul of Samosata,
bishop of Antioch in the third century, who was condemned for
keeping young virgins as disciples in his house. Some other
canonical legislation suggests this interpretation and it seems the
most likely. A few scholars, however, see it as an early insistence
on clerical celibacy.

The main topic of the next four canons is the episcopate.
Canon 4 urges that before a bishop is ordained, all the existing
bishops of the province should give their written consent, and
preferably all of them, or at least three, should attend the ordination. This is another aspect of the concern for unanimity or
general consent that was mentioned in connection with the
creeds. A bishop, especially in the new era of official status given
to the church by Emperor Constantine, was a public figure, and
it was important to know who the bishops were and that they
had been ordained correctly. Canon 5 is about excommunications issued by bishops and their holding councils twice a year
in each province. These regular local councils remind us that
government in the church at this time was fundamentally conciliar. Canons 6 and 7 speak of a three-tiered hierarchy within
the episcopate: bishops, metropolitans, and at the top the great
sees of Rome, Alexandria, and Antioch—later to be joined by
Constantinople and Jerusalem and to be called patriarchates—

which are accorded an unspecified "authority" over their regions.

Most of the next seven canons, 8 to 14, concern people who lapsed in time of persecution. This was a burning issue of the day inasmuch as the conversion of Emperor Constantine to Christianity, and the consequent toleration given to Christians, had been preceded by several fierce persecutions, notably under Emperor Diocletian beginning in 303 and under Licinius, who was co-emperor with Constantine for a time and struggled for power with him. Throughout these canons there is a spirit of reconciliation, but rather more severity is shown toward clergy who had lapsed than to lay people.

The process of reconciliation was often through public penance. Three grades of penitents are mentioned, all in the context of the Eucharist: "hearers," who were allowed to hear the liturgy of the word and then had to depart; "prostrators," who, after the liturgy of the word, received a blessing from the president, for which they prostrated themselves, and then departed; finally "prayers," who remained throughout the eucharistic prayer but did not receive communion. People lived in a public and community-oriented world, so that open penance for notorious offenses seemed appropriate. Often the period of penance may appear long. Soldiers who had enlisted in the anti-Christian army of Licinius, for example, had to spend three years as "hearers" and ten as "prostrators" (canon 12); but the bishop could dispense them altogether from their time as prostrators and "decide even more favourably in their regard." There are other indications, too, that justice was tempered with mercy.

Canons 15 and 16 concern stability of the clergy. They forbid bishops, priests, and deacons to transfer from one city or diocese to another and they forbid bishops to poach clergy from other dioceses. In these canons, too, we can see the new situation created by the establishment of Christianity as the privileged religion of the Roman Empire and its consequent dangers, especially the opportunities for clerical careerism. The prohibition against bishops moving from one see to another, which usually meant promotion to a larger and more important see, was soon forgotten. Canon 17 forbids clergy to engage in usury, and 18 reminds deacons that their liturgical rank is below that of both bishops and priests.

Canon 19 is interesting on account of the great importance it appears to attach to correct teaching about the Trinity—understandably so since this teaching was central to the creed of the same council—and because it mentions deaconesses. The canon is concerned with reconciling followers of Paul of Samosata, who was mentioned earlier in connection with canon 3. In this case the issue in question, though it is not explicitly stated in the canon, was almost certainly the inadequacy of his teaching on the Trinity, not his practice of cohabiting with women. His followers who wished to be reconciled with the Catholic Church are told that they must be rebaptized unconditionally, presumably because a faulty understanding of the Trinity rendered their previous Baptisms not just irregular but invalid. Deaconesses are mentioned obliquely in the context of this reconciliation, and the canon makes clear that they are to be regarded as lay women. In canon 15 of the Council of Chalcedon, however, there is clear reference to the ordination of women as deacons [A-T, p. 94], and this canon is the main reason why, in the current debate on the ordination of women, Rome is careful to restrict its prohibition to the ordination of women as priests and bishops and not to rule out the possibility of their ordination as deacons.

Finally, canon 20 forbids kneeling "on Sundays and during the season of Pentecost" (i.e., Eastertide in modern parlance, from Easter to Pentecost) and asks Christians at these times to "offer their prayers to the Lord standing." Sundays and Eastertide are times when the Lord's resurrection is specially remembered, and standing is more symbolic of resurrection than kneeling. Possibly, too, the canon did not wish to risk confusion with Christians who were undergoing penance and as a result had to kneel. It is fascinating to note the changing attitudes to bodily posture in prayer through the centuries.

A few points may be noted in conclusion. Like the creed of Nicaea, the twenty canons were not made up by the council from nothing; many of them are known to have been based on the canons of earlier, local councils or of other canonical collections [A-T, pp. 6–16, gives the references]. They presuppose, too, like the other disciplinary canons of the early councils, a life and practice within the church; they are, as it were, ideals and interpretations within this lived experience, not an iron code imposed from outside or from above. They were not meant to be a comprehensive code covering all aspects of canon law, such as the 1917 and 1983 codes of the Roman Catholic Church. Rather they touch on particular points that seemed to need attention. More about their composition is hard to say from our relatively scanty knowledge of the council. They come down to us principally through the sixth-century collection of canons compiled by John Scholasticus, patriarch of Constantinople, and in their Latin translation through a slightly earlier collection made by Dionysius Exiguus. They form the most influential canonical collection of the early church and are essential for any understanding of the "church order" dimension of councils.

Other Councils

Two other councils should be considered because of their claims to ecumenical status: the Council of Trullo and the Fourth Council of Constantinople.

The Council of Trullo—often called the Trullan synod or the council in Trullo—met in the domed room (τροῦλλος) of

Emperor Justinian II's palace in Constantinople in 692. It promulgated an extensive collection of 102 canons, and in canon 2
it listed the earlier canonical authorities that were to be followed
[2a, Nedungatt and Featherstone, 1995, pp. 41–186, for the
canons and an English translation]. Thus it provided a code that
has remained the basis of canon law in the eastern churches ever
since. In the East it is regarded as the continuation of the sixth
ecumenical council, Constantinople III of 680–681, or sometimes as the completion of the fifth (Constantinople II of 553)
and sixth councils—hence its alternative names of the "Quini-
sext" or "fifth-sixth" council—inasmuch as it provided disciplinary canons which these two councils lacked.

Several canons caused problems for Rome, for example 13,
28, 55, 57, and 82, which are critical of various practices of the
Roman church, and canon 36, which sanctions the pentarchy of
five more or less autonomous patriarchates of Rome, Constantinople, Alexandria, Antioch, and Jerusalem, and decrees that
the see of Constantinople "is to enjoy privileges equal to those
of the see of older Rome and to be magnified as it is in ecclesiastical affairs, coming second after it." These difficulties do not
seem automatically to disqualify the council from ecumenical
status since some statements of other councils that are generally
recognized as ecumenical were distasteful to Rome, for example,
the condemnations of Pope Honorius mentioned earlier or
Chalcedon's canon 28 on the prerogatives of the see of Constantinople. The council certainly regarded itself as ecumenical,
and it enjoyed a measure of acceptance as such in the West. Subsequently and for a long time it was omitted from the lists of
ecumenical councils in the West, but in recent years many western scholars have urged that the council fulfills the criteria,
including adequate confirmation of it in the West, to be
regarded as ecumenical [N. Dură in 2a, Nedungatt and Featherstone, 1995, pp. 239–62]. The issue is important, especially in
view of the significance of many of the canons, including canon

13, which recognizes married clergy. Though the purpose of the council was primarily to legislate for the eastern church, or for the regions that lay within the jurisdiction of Emperor Justinian II, rather than for the West, so that even if the council is regarded as ecumenical, the relevance of its canons to the western church may be limited.

The Fourth Council of Constantinople is, in many ways, an opposite case. That is to say, although it was for long accepted as an ecumenical council in the West, it was quickly rejected as such in the East. Meeting in 869–870, its principal business was to confirm the deposition of Photius, patriarch of Constantinople, which had been initiated by the eastern emperor and approved by the pope shortly beforehand: the council used strongly critical language of the patriarch and his supporters. Photius was later reinstated as patriarch and is venerated as a saint in the eastern church. A letter of disputed authenticity allegedly written by the next pope, John VII, to the eastern emperor a decade later in 879 approved the reinstatement of Photius and annulled the proceedings of the council. The case in favor of the ecumenicity of the council, which appears in some western lists of ecumenical councils from the twelfth century onward, partly depends on the assumption that the papal letter of 879 is spurious. In recent years, however, the consensus of western scholars has been that the letter is genuine and for this reason, in addition to the rejection of the council in the East, the council cannot be regarded as ecumenical [2a, Peri, 1976, pp. 52–79]. It is now time for the Roman Catholic Church to recognize its error more officially, I would suggest, and thereby to remove the offense felt by the eastern church on account of the western church's long acceptance of the council as ecumenical. It should be remembered, however, that the dispute was originally and principally within the eastern church and empire, the western church being drawn into the dispute only reluctantly in the early stages.

Conclusion

The ecumenical councils are the highest peaks of a vast mountain range. Some of the foothills have been glimpsed already. Many of the disciplinary canons of the ecumenical councils were based on canons of earlier local councils, as we saw in the case of Nicaea I. Likewise with the creeds and other doctrinal statements, the issues had been discussed beforehand in local councils. Canon 5 of Nicaea I, mentioned earlier, which required councils to be held twice a year in each province, gives some idea of how extensive was this interlocking network of conciliar discussion and decision making. Mansi and numerous subsequent and more critical editions of local councils, as well as the great secondary work by the German and French scholars K. J. Hefele and H. Leclerq [1, Hefele and Leclerq, 1907–52], provide the basic knowledge about this intermediate level of councils, though even they are providing, for the most part, only a skeleton outline of what was actually going on.

How far and wide do we go? Council (or synod) can mean any gathering for discussion, however informal, and there seems to have been plenty of discussion at the grass roots level in the early church. Gregory of Nyssa gives us an idea of this, speaking of the popular debate about the Trinity that went on in Constantinople shortly after the council there in 381: "If in this city you ask anyone for change, he will discuss with you whether the Son is begotten or unbegotten; if you ask about the quality of bread, you will receive the answer that the Father is greater, the Son is less; if you suggest you require a bath, you will be told that there was nothing before the Son was created!" [*PG*, 46, col. 557]. Any understanding of the ecumenical councils of the early church requires some knowledge of other councils, but to enter into this topic properly requires another book and more!

It is naive to be too starry-eyed about the councils of the early church. There were many difficulties. Yet the fact remains

that in many ways the church was then considerably more consultative than it became later. Christians, therefore, need not fear
the more consultative model of the church encouraged in our
own time by Vatican II: rather than a dangerous innovation, it is
a conservative return to earlier practices.

It is noticeable that these remarkable councils took place in
a time of great political turmoil. In the West the Roman Empire
succumbed to the invasions of various so-called barbarian tribes;
the eastern empire, although it survived, was under threat from
similar invaders and later from the spread of Islam. North Africa
was largely lost to Christianity. Just as some of the finest works
of the Old Testament were written during the Babylonian Cap-
tivity and Christ lived during the Roman occupation of his land,
so the principal decrees of the early councils after Nicaea I
emerged in a time of political crisis and humiliation. To what
extent there is cause and effect the reader may decide, but the
paradox at least gives hope for life and creativity in other times
of apparent disaster.

The early councils are also a tribute to unity in the church,
with some important qualifications. Nestorians were unable to
accept the Council of Ephesus and broke away; monophysites
likewise over Chalcedon, and there were other splits. Relations
between Rome and Constantinople, the principal sees of the
western and eastern churches, were frequently tense, and there
were periods of schism. Yet the main body of the church
remained in communion, owing in good measure to the working of the councils.

CHAPTER TWO

Medieval Councils:
Lateran I to Lateran V

Introduction

Between the schism of the eastern and western churches beginning in the eleventh century and the further divisions within the western church resulting from the Reformation in the sixteenth century, ten councils have found their place in the Roman Catholic Church's traditional list of ecumenical and general councils: Lateran I (1123), Lateran II (1139), Lateran III (1179), Lateran IV (1215), Lyons I (1245), Lyons II (1274), Vienne (1311–1312), Constance (1414–1418), Basel-Florence (1431–1445), and Lateran V (1512–1517).

The first point to note is the very changed situation. More than three centuries elapsed between Nicaea II in 787, the last generally recognized ecumenical council before the schism, and Lateran I in 1123—an exceptionally long gap during which many changes had occurred. The beginning of the schism is often dated to 1054, when excommunications were exchanged between Rome and Constantinople after a period of considerable tension; though other dates may be preferred. For long the hope was that the schism would be healed, just as previous disputes had been resolved, but in fact this was not to be so and the schism hardened, notably after the sack of Constantinople by western crusaders in 1204. Radical changes resulted for the councils.

Thus, whereas the seven councils from Nicaea I to Nicaea II were held within the eastern church, all those from Lateran I in 1123 to Lateran V in 1512–1517 were held in western Europe: the five Lateran councils in the palace or basilica of the Lateran in Rome, two councils in Lyons in France, one in Vienne, a papal fief which lay within the Holy Roman Empire though geographically it formed part of southern France, one in Constance in southern Germany, and one was held partly in Basel in Switzerland and partly in Florence in Italy.

There was a corresponding change in the provenance of the participants. That is to say, whereas at the early councils the large majority of the participants came from the East, significant contingents from North Africa, and very few from the West, at the medieval councils the overwhelming majority of participants were of the western church. On account of the schism, the eastern church was not represented apart from a small delegation at the Council of Lyons II and a rather larger one at the Council of Florence, who took part in the negotiations for reunion with the western church at the two councils. Islam's dominance of North Africa meant that very few representatives of this region attended.

The primary language of the councils and of the decrees they promulgated changed from Greek, the language of the eastern church, to Latin, the language of the West. The role of the eastern emperor, in summoning the council, presiding over it either in person or through representatives, and promulgating its decrees, was largely taken over by the bishop of Rome, the pope. There was, too, a marked change of interest. That is to say, whereas doctrinal statements were the most important features of the early councils and disciplinary decrees were of secondary importance, in the medieval councils the emphasis was reversed.

What, therefore, is the status of these medieval councils?

The Orthodox Church, the oriental churches, and the churches of the Reformation do not accept them as ecumenical councils. The Orthodox Church accepts as ecumenical only the first seven councils from Nicaea I to Nicaea II in 787 and does not extend this list to include the medieval councils for the obvious reason that it was not represented at them in any full sense. The oriental churches vary in their attitude to the early councils, but they agree with the Orthodox Church with regard to the medieval councils. The churches of the Reformation vary in their attitude toward the authority of councils as a whole, but none of them, it seems clear, would extend the list of ecumenical councils beyond Nicaea II, both because the later councils lacked the participation of the eastern church and because they tend to reject the authority of the medieval church in general, and therefore its councils, on the grounds that it was in a state of radical error.

What about the attitude of the Roman Catholic Church? The question is of great importance for two reasons: first, on account of the authority that should be given to the decrees of these councils within the Roman Catholic Church; second and consequently, on account of the authority to be given to them in its dialogues with other churches. So many of the issues in dispute between the Roman Catholic Church, on the one hand, and the Orthodox Church and the churches of the Reformation, on the other, hang on statements made by these councils, and therefore the attitude to their authority is crucial to the discussions and the possibilities of reunion.

The answer, however, is not simple. Medieval people themselves in western Christendom were uncertain about the status of their own councils, and the clear weight of opinion was that they were not ecumenical. The point is brought out clearly in the profession of faith that the Council of Constance in 1415 required of a future pope. In listing the councils that the pope should respect, the profession drew a distinction between the eight "holy universal/ecumenical" (Latin, *universalia*) councils from Nicaea I to Constantinople IV and the "general" (Latin, *generalia*) councils at the Lateran, Lyons, and Vienne [below, p. 68]. The distinction is not expanded upon, but it is evident that some difference in status is intended. Other evidence showing that most of the medieval councils were not then regarded as ecumenical, mainly from the fifteenth and early sixteenth centuries, has been summarized by Victor Peri and Luis Bermejo [1, Peri, 1963, pp. 473–75; 1, Bermejo, 1990, pp. 77–78]. In particular, the Council of Florence was often referred to, including by popes and their legates, as the eighth or ninth ecumenical council: that is, coming immediately after Nicaea II or Constantinople IV and excluding the earlier medieval councils. It was thought impossible to have an ecumenical council without the participation of the eastern church.

The attempt to promote the medieval councils to ecumenical status came about during the Counter-Reformation. Roman Catholic apologists sought to defend the true church as they saw it against the attacks of the Reformation by an appeal to its medieval heritage, and the councils from Lateran I to Lateran V formed an important part of this heritage. Robert Bellarmine, the Jesuit theologian, and Cesare Baronius, the Oratorian scholar, both cardinals, were influential in the development, and so was as the publication of the "Roman edition" of the councils, mentioned earlier [above pp. 7–8]. The edition gave to the medieval councils the same status as those of the early church, calling them all "ecumenical" in the Greek part of the book's title and "general" in the Latin part, thus cleverly sliding over the possible distinction between the two words. It drew up a list of nineteen councils: the seven generally accepted councils of the undivided church from Nicaea I to Nicaea II, Constantinople IV, the ten medieval councils from Lateran I to Lateran V (excluding the Basel part of Basel-Florence), and Trent. The list came to be widely accepted within the Roman Catholic Church, and all the councils were normally called "ecumenical" rather than "general." The list gained for a time a semi-official status, though the matter was never defined in an authoritative way.

The issue has been reopened in recent times. The year 1974 saw two important contributions. First, the influential Dominican theologian Yves Congar wrote a wide-ranging article on criteria for ecumenicity in councils, in which he questioned the list of twenty-one ecumenical councils (the nineteen from Nicaea I to Trent plus Vatican I and II) that had become traditional within the Roman Catholic Church [1, Congar, 1974, pp. 355–90]. Second, as part of the celebrations of the seventh centenary of the Second Council of Lyons in 1274, Pope Paul VI wrote a letter to Cardinal Willebrands, president of the Secretariat for Christian Unity, in which he referred to Lyons II and the earlier medieval councils as "general councils of the West" (*generales synodos in occidentali orbe*) rather than as ecumenical councils, a choice of language that is significant and appears intended [*AAS*, vol. 66, 1974, p. 620]. Since 1974 there has been some further discussion of the issue, though not as much as might have been expected in view of its possible fruitfulness. There has been a general tendency even within the Roman Catholic communion to follow the lead of Paul VI and call the medieval councils "general councils of the western church" rather than cling to the ecumenical title for them. The Anglican-Roman Catholic International Commission (ARCIC) touched briefly on the issue in its first "Agreed Statement on Authority in the Church" (1976), no. 19, mentioning obliquely the distinction between ecumenical and general councils, but disappointingly it did not develop the argument.

The question of whether the ten medieval councils from Lateran I to Lateran V are to be regarded as general councils of the western church rather than ecumenical councils is undoubtedly an important one. But even as general councils they are of great significance. They were the most authoritative councils in western Christendom, and it was in western Christendom that the large majority of Christians lived. Certainly there was still vitality in the eastern church, and councils continued there into the modern era—for example, the Councils of Constantinople in 1341 and 1351, which endorsed Hesychasm, and the Councils of Jassy in 1642 and Jerusalem in 1672, which taught concerning the Eucharist and the nature of the church—but with the advance of Islam it was for the most part a church on the defensive, and developments were limited. Islam's continuing dominance of North Africa meant there was, sadly, little contribution from this region. Another point is that the subsequent general councils of the Roman Catholic Church, namely Trent, Vatican I, and Vatican II, undoubtedly saw themselves as being in continuity with the medieval councils of western Christendom. Despite the gravely flawed nature of the church following the East-West schism in the eleventh century, it may reasonably be argued that the mainstream of life and development in the church moved gradually and for many centuries to western Christendom, and the councils from Lateran I to Lateran V formed the central core of conciliar development during the first half of this western period. When a schism occurs the church cannot stand still; the clock cannot be stopped; development continues within a fragmented situation.

Papal Councils: Lateran I to Vienne

The first seven general councils, from Lateran I in 1123 to Vienne in 1311–1312, may be described as papal councils inasmuch as the summons, the presiding over them, and the promulgation of the decrees were all carried out by the pope either in person or through officials. In general, moreover, the decrees appear to have been prepared by the pope and his curia before the council assembled, so that the work of the council was largely to rubber-stamp this prepared legislation. Precision on this point is impossible to attain because the relevant evidence is often lacking. Other factors certainly played a part. In the case of Vienne, for example, the king of France, Philip the Fair, exerted much pressure on Pope Clement V in the composition of the council's decrees: at Lyons I, Pope Innocent IV's desire, ultimately successful, to include a decree deposing Emperor Frederick was vigorously contested by some prelates from Germany; and at other councils there is evidence of debate over and amendments to some decrees. On the whole, however, it is clear that the decrees were prepared beforehand, rather than emerging from debate within the council as had usually been the case in the early councils.

To understand the decrees one really needs to read them! They cannot easily be summarized. They are extraordinarily interesting and have something to say on almost every aspect of life in the medieval church. Indeed they provide an unrivalled insight into medieval Christianity. The best introduction to them is provided by a look at the decrees of the Fourth Lateran Council of 1215 [A-T, pp. 227–71]. This was the most important of the seven general councils in question and the most wideranging in scope. It may be described as the Trent or Vatican II of the Middle Ages.

It met in November 1215, having been summoned by Pope Innocent III for this purpose: "to eradicate vices and to plant virtues, to correct faults and to reform morals, to remove heresies and to strengthen faith, to settle discords and to establish peace, to get rid of oppression and to foster liberty, to induce princes and Christian people to come to the aid and succour of the Holy Land." Over four hundred bishops from throughout western Christendom attended in addition to other representatives of church and state. There were just three solemn sessions: an opening session on November 11, a second one nine days later at which the competing claims of Frederick II and Otto IV to be recognized as Holy Roman Emperor were debated with much feeling, and a final one on November 30 at which the seventy-one decrees of the council were read out and approved. It seems clear that in substance the decrees had been drawn up by Pope Innocent and his curia before the beginning of the council, though some decrees appear to have been subject to discussion and some amendment during the course of the council. Moreover, the local councils that Innocent had asked to take place throughout Christendom in preparation for the Lateran council probably influenced the pope and curia in their drafting of the decrees, though it is difficult to be precise on this point. Some idea of the council's concerns is provided by the headings of the decrees, which are as follows:

1. The catholic faith
2. Error of Abbot Joachim
3. Heretics
4. Pride of Greeks toward Latins
5. Dignity of patriarchs
6. Provincial councils
7. Correction of offenses
8. Inquests
9. Different rites within the same faith
10. Appointing preachers
11. Schoolmasters
12. General chapters of monks
13. Prohibition against new religious orders
14. Punishing clerical incontinence
15. Preventing drunkenness among the clergy
16. Dress of clerics
17. Prelates' feasts and their negligence at divine services
18. Sentences involving either the shedding of blood or a duel are forbidden to clerics
19. Profane objects may not be introduced into churches
20. Keeping chrism and the Eucharist under lock and key

21. On confession being made, and not revealed by the priest, and on communicating at least at Easter
22. The sick should provide for the soul before the body
23. A cathedral church or a church of the regular clergy is not to remain vacant for more than three months
24. Making an election by ballot or by agreement
25. An election made by a secular power is invalid
26. Penalty for improperly confirming an election
27. Instruction of ordinands
28. Those who have asked for permission to resign are to be compelled to do so
29. Nobody may hold two benefices with the cure of souls attached
30. Suitability of those instituted to churches
31. Not instituting the sons of canons with their fathers
32. Patrons shall leave a suitable portion to clerics
33. Not receiving procurations without a visitation being made
34. Not burdening subjects under the pretext of some service
35. Stating the grounds for an appeal
36. A judge can revoke an interlocutory and a comminatory sentence
37. Not procuring letters which entail more than two days' journey and are without a special mandate
38. Writing acts so that they can be proved
39. Granting restitution against a person in possession who was not the robber
40. True possession
41. Continuing good faith in every prescription
42. Secular justice
43. On a cleric not doing fealty to a layman without good reason
44. Ordinances of princes should not be prejudicial to churches

45. A patron who kills or mutilates a cleric of a church loses his right of patronage
46. Not exacting taxes from clerics
47. Form of excommunication
48. How to challenge a judge
49. Punishment for excommunicating someone unjustly
50. Restriction of prohibitions to matrimony
51. Punishment of those who contract clandestine marriages
52. Rejecting evidence from hearsay in a matrimonial suit
53. On those who give their fields to others to be cultivated so as to avoid paying tithes
54. Tithes should be paid before taxes
55. Tithes are to be paid on lands that are acquired, notwithstanding privileges
56. A parish priest shall not lose tithes on account of some people making a pact
57. Interpreting the words of privileges
58. The same in favor of bishops
59. No religious may give surety without the permission of his abbot and convent
60. Abbots should not encroach on the episcopal office
61. Religious may not receive tithes from lay hands
62. Saints' relics may not be exhibited outside reliquaries, nor may newly discovered relics be venerated without authorization from the Roman church
63. Simony
64. The same with regard to monks and nuns
65. The same with regard to the illegal extortion of money
66. The same with regard to the avarice of clerics
67. Usury of Jews
68. Jews should be distinguished from Christians in their dress
69. Jews are not to hold public offices

70. Converts to the faith among Jews may not retain their old
    rite
71. Expedition for the recovery of the Holy Land

It is notable that only decrees 1–2 are concerned with doctrine and theology; all the rest are disciplinary in nature: a rever-
sal of the early councils. The paucity of doctrinal decrees does
not mean at all that medieval people were uninterested in theology. Rather, speculative thought of this kind was done largely
outside councils, in other forums, notably in the universities,
where it was indulged in with passion.

The first decree is a creed. Directed especially against
Catharism, a dualist heresy that saw the material world as evil
and formed probably the most serious threat to orthodox Christianity at the time, it is less elegant than the Nicene-Constantinopolitan creed of 381 and never replaced it. Its final paragraph
is indicative of the great importance that was attached to membership in the visible church, "There is one universal church of
the faithful outside of which nobody at all is saved," it begins:
strong words that were to cause problems at Vatican II. The
ensuing defense of the sacraments, which were attacked by
Cathars because they used material objects, contains the first
mention of transubstantiation in a conciliar decree to describe
the change involved in the Eucharist. Decree 2, the only other
doctrinal decree, need not detain us, involving as it does a rather
abstruse controversy about the nature of the Trinity between
Joachim of Fiore and Peter Lombard.

The third decree, "On heretics," is very important for
understanding the medieval sense of a Christian society. "We
excommunicate and anathematize every heresy raising itself up
against this holy, orthodox and catholic faith which we have
expounded above. We condemn all heretics, whatever names
they may go under. They have different faces indeed but their
tails are tied together inasmuch as they are alike in their pride.

Let those condemned be handed over to the secular authorities present . . . for due punishment." Membership of the church was regarded as vital for salvation, as the first decree stated, and being part of a Christian society was normally a corollary to membership of the church. Another point is the sense that the Christian message is self-evidently true, so that anyone who has seen the light and then rejects it must be gravely at fault: hence the equating of heresy with pride.

The fourth decree, "On the pride of Greeks towards Latins," is another decree that we may find difficult to stomach today. Western crusaders had sacked Constantinople only a decade earlier in 1204, yet there is no remorse or apology, only placing the blame for the schism between the two churches on the Greeks. The medieval West had a passionate concern for truth and right living, usually in justification of its own teaching and behavior. The dark side was intolerance and self-righteousness, but the brighter side was creativity. Much of the inventiveness of the medieval West in religion, as in other areas of life, arose out of this passion for truth and life, and without it much of the originality would have been lost.

Another undercurrent is the inferiority complex of the West. From the sixteenth century onward Christianity developed into a world religion with an accompanying confidence and often arrogance. The Middle Ages predates that development. At that time Christianity, more particularly western Christendom, occupied a small corner of the globe, and in many ways it was a shrinking religion. Islam and the Tartars threatened its very existence, as the Second Council of Lyons in 1245, just four years after the Tartars had captured and sacked the city of Budapest in Hungary, bemoaned in its decree "The Tartars": "When—God forbid!—the world is bereaved of the faithful, faith may turn aside from the world to lament its followers destroyed by the barbarity of this people" [A-T, p. 297]. Besides the physical threats, four civilizations were felt in various ways to be superior to Christendom: the classical world of ancient Rome, with which the medieval West had in many respects never really caught up; Byzantium, which considered itself to be the true heir of the ancient world much more than its upstart barbarian neighbors in the West; Islam, with its spectacular religious and material successes; and Judaism, a much older religion than Christianity whose adherents excelled Christians in many walks of life.

Decree 4 of Lateran IV directs attention to the second of these perceived religious and cultural threats, Byzantium. But it provides an opportunity to consider the wider question of the West's defensiveness at this time, which lies just below the surface of other decrees: hence the above semidigression. The relevant point is that pastoral care at this time meant care of a religion and a society that were perceived to be fragile. Many decrees of the council appear aggressive and uncaring, but they should also be seen as the rather clumsy instincts or panic reactions of people who felt threatened, of people who cared for and wished to preserve what was precious to them. They express, too, an underlying sense of guilt: that Christians were to blame for the fact that Christianity wasn't doing better in spreading the faith and converting people.

Decrees 5–6 and 9 keep contact with the organization of the early church. The five patriarchates of Rome, Constantinople, Alexandria, Antioch, and Jerusalem are preserved, though it is little more than a "paper constitution" inasmuch as Rome's claims to authority over the other four sees were quite unacceptable to the eastern church, and anyway three of the cities—Alexandria, Antioch, and Jerusalem—were out of Christian control and in the hands of Islam. The holding of regular provincial and diocesan councils reminds us of the vast network of councils at the local level, though here too there is a major change from the early church, inasmuch as these councils are seen much more in terms of executing and transmitting the decisions of general councils, a "from above" approach rather than the more "grass-roots" or "from below" activity of earlier councils. Even so, the medieval church was in many ways more democratic and pluralist—"corporate" is the better word—than the Roman Catholic Church is today.

The concerns of the remaining decrees may be divided into the following: the clergy and religious orders; the laity; non-Christians. There is considerable overlap especially between the first and second topics.

Many decrees touch on the life-style of the clergy. Their chastity (14), eating and drinking (15), dress (16), occupations forbidden to them (18) are topics treated. Many decrees try to ensure the provision of suitable pastors for churches; many are concerned with legal procedures. The education and training of the clergy are discussed in 11, which provided for teachers in cathedral churches, and more generally in 27, "On the instruction of ordinands." Religious orders are mentioned several times, and there is a prohibition against founding new ones in decree 13, which reflects nervousness about the emerging orders of Franciscan and Dominican friars. The responsibilities of the clergy toward the laity feature in various decrees: preaching (10), taking proper care of the churches in their charge (19–20), and indirectly in many others.

Of the decrees touching more directly on the laity, decree 21, on annual confession and communion, was influential. While reception of both sacraments was recommended before this time, the obligation for people to receive them annually, "after they have reached the age of discernment," was created by the decree. A loophole was provided regarding communion, if "they think, for a good reason and on the advice of their own (parish) priest, that they should abstain from receiving it for a time"; and regarding confession, friars were soon given permission to take the place of the individual's parish priest as the confessor, often to the irritation of the latter. In other respects the decree was comprehensive. Richard Helmslay, a witty English Dominican friar from Newcastle-upon-Tyne, later argued from the opening words of the decree, which read "All the faithful of both sexes" (*Omnis utriusque sexus*), that it applied only to her-maphrodites, but he was roundly condemned and obliged to make a public recantation in both Newcastle-upon-Tyre and Durham [2b, Pantin, 1955, pp. 164–65]!

An intriguing decree is 22, which indicates the tension between official attitudes and popular approaches. "Physicians of the body" are told, "when they are called to the sick, to warn and persuade them first to call in physicians of the soul, so that after their spiritual health has been seen to they may respond better to medicine for their bodies; for when the cause ceases so does the effect"; the argument is accepted that "sickness of the body may sometimes be the result of sin." The paramountcy of the spiritual over the bodily is reinforced in the final sentence: "Moreover, since the soul is much more precious than the body, we forbid any physician, under pain of anathema, to prescribe anything for the bodily health of a sick person that may endan-ger his soul." The supposed dangers to the soul are not spelled out, but the use by physicians of astrology, charms, magical potions, and such may well have been in mind. Many of the best doctors, moreover, were Jews, and there was suspicion of them in some quarters. Another reason was given later by Boniface Ferrer, former prior-general of the Carthusians and brother of St. Vincent Ferrer. He thought that doctors were urging greater and irregular indulgence in sex as a cure for bodily ailments [2b, Ferrer, chapter 36].

Four decrees concern marriage. At the end of the first decree, the creed, there had been muted praise for wives and husbands (albeit in a somewhat condescending manner): "For not only virgins and the continent but also married persons find favour with God by right faith and good actions and deserve to attain to eternal blessedness." Decrees 50–52 touch on various specific issues. In decree 50 the number of degrees of consanguinity (relationship by blood) and affinity (various other relationships, e.g., by marriage, through godparents) within which marriage was prohibited were reduced from seven to four. The reasons given for the reduction are revealing: "since God changed in the New Testament some of the commandments of the Old Testament," therefore human laws can be changed "when urgent necessity or evident advantage demands it." The decree implicitly admits that the previous rules were not being observed: a reminder in general that laws should not be taken too seriously and that the legislation of Lateran IV, indeed that of the whole medieval church, was the result of pressure "from below" and was not simply enacted from on high. Four, the number of degrees still prohibited, was chosen because "there are four humours in the body, which is composed of the four elements" (earth, air, fire, and water), an intriguing line of thought that was not explained!

Decree 51 sought to prohibit secret (or "clandestine") marriages: "When marriages are to be contracted they shall be announced publicly in the churches by priests, with a suitable time being fixed beforehand within which whoever wishes and is able to may adduce a lawful impediment." The advantages of knowing clearly who were married and who were not were obvious to both church and state, even though in practice many people preferred cohabitation or a somewhat ambiguous marital status. Decree 52 gives procedures for disputed cases about consanguinity and affinity, ending with a tolerant instruction: "It is better to leave alone some people who have been united contrary to human decrees than to separate, contrary to the Lord's decrees, persons who have been joined together legitimately."

Relations between the laity and clergy feature in various decrees on lay patronage of benefices—the rights of the laity in various offices of the church—in, for example, the appointment and revenues for parish priests (25, 32, 45), taxation of the clergy (46), payment of tithes (53–56), and the distinction between secular and ecclesiastical justice (42, 43). The two swords, the spiritual belonging to the church, the temporal belonging to secular rulers, are summed up in decree 42, with generous autonomy for the latter: "Just as we desire lay people not to usurp the rights of clerics, so we ought to wish clerics not to lay claim to the rights of the laity. We therefore forbid every cleric henceforth to extend his jurisdiction, under pretext of ecclesiastical freedom, to the prejudice of secular justice. Rather let him be satisfied with the written constitutions and customs hitherto approved, so that the things of Caesar may be rendered unto Caesar and the things of God may be rendered unto God by a right distribution."

Relations with the non-Christian world focus on four decrees on Jews (67–70) and the final decree on the crusade (71). The decrees on Jews are among the most problematic. The titles alone indicate the hostile tone: "Usury of Jews," "Jews must be distinguished from Christians in their dress,' "Jews may not hold public offices," "Converts to the faith among Jews may not retain their old rite." Jewish money-lending is called a "perfidy" by which Christians are "savagely oppressed." Jews are ordered to wear distinctive dress, and they are forbidden to enter marriages with Christians, which are described as a "damnable mixing." They were forbidden to hold public offices since "it is absurd for a blasphemer of Christ to exercise power over Christians," and Jewish converts to Christianity were to be prevented by a "salutary and necessary coercion" from returning to Judaism. The measures were intended to protect Christians from Jews, resulting partly from the sense of unease and inferiority toward Judaism, which has already been mentioned. Belief in the virtues of a Christian society was also influential. Nevertheless, the decrees are a sad deviation and show that Christianity can go badly wrong when it becomes over-zealous.

The council's last decree, on the crusade to the Holy Land, was intended to be the climax of all the others, the culmination of the reforms initiated by them. A reformed church in a united Christendom would be able to undertake the crusade to recapture Jerusalem and other parts of the Holy Land that had fallen to Islam. "It is our ardent desire to liberate the Holy Land from infidel hands," the decree begins, and it goes on to describe the enterprise as "this work of Jesus Christ" (*negotium Iesu Christi*). Crusades were a prominent feature of medieval Christendom, and decrees similar to Lateran IV's were issued by several other general councils [A-T, pp. 297–301, 309–12, 350–54, 609–14, and 650–55]. The councils' promotion of this form of holy war is one of the most serious and sustained errors in the history of the church.

How do we sum up the Fourth Lateran Council? It is not a council about which one can remain neutral. On the one hand, heretics are condemned; Jews are threatened; warfare encouraged; and the Spirit is stifled by the prohibition against new religious orders. On the other hand, there is a passionate concern for truth, that human beings reach their divine destiny, and great attention to the means to this end. Any attempt to understand the history of the western church has to come to terms with this council. It issued a decree of some relevance in almost all the areas of Christian life in a period that saw spectacular achievements, as well as deviations and disasters: famous saints such as Francis and Clare of Assisi or King Louis IX of France; the four orders of friars of Franciscans, Dominicans, Carmelites, and Augustinians; the beguine movement for women; the universities, notably Bologna, Paris, and Oxford; theologians of the stature of Thomas Aquinas and Duns Scotus; mystical writers such as Hadewijch, Mechtild of Magdeburg, and Gertrude the Great; parish churches, cathedrals, and works of art; the Christianity of countless individuals, largely unknown; as well as the

Inquisition, crusades, continuing schism with the eastern church, the expulsion of Jews. The council, of course, did not produce all these results, but at least it was participating in events and was not just a spectator of them.

Constance, Basel-Florence, and Lateran V

Of the last three general councils of the pre-Reformation period, Constance and Basel-Florence witnessed a great constitutional crisis in the church.

The background to the crisis is relatively simple to narrate and fiercely contested in its interpretation. For almost seventy years, from 1309 to 1377, the popes lived at Avignon, which was the principal city in lands belonging to the papacy in southern France. Within months of returning to Rome in January 1378, the reigning pope, Gregory XI, died and there followed a disputed election. The Roman populace pressed the cardinals to elect a citizen of Rome as pope, fearing that if someone else or at least a non-Italian was chosen he might return to Avignon. Eventually an Italian, though not a Roman, was chosen, Bartholomew Prignano, archbishop of Bari, who took the name of Urban VI. Was the pressure of the Roman crowd sufficient to invalidate his election? That was the great question that rapidly divided western Christendom. For a few weeks Urban was recognized as pope by the cardinals, but he rapidly showed himself very overbearing and abusive toward them and many other people. Within a few months the cardinals declared the election invalid on the grounds of the undue pressure of the Roman populace, deposed Urban as pope, and elected in his place Robert of Geneva, who took the name of Clement VII. Clement soon moved to Avignon, Urban remained in Rome, each establishing his own papal court and college of cardinals. Christendom divided in its allegiance: northern Italy, Germany, central Europe, Scandinavia, and England, for the most part, were

Urbanite; France, Spain, and Scotland were Clementine; some territories were divided in their allegiance, others switched from one loyalty to another. Saints, too, differed: Catherine of Siena was a fierce supporter of Urban; Vincent of Ferrer was equally convinced of Clement's claims.

The schism lasted some forty years, with a succession of popes being elected for each of the two lines. Early on a council was suggested as the best means to resolve the crisis, but it was not until 1409, after attempts to persuade the two popes to resign had collapsed, that the two colleges of cardinals called the Council of Pisa. The council deposed the two popes and elected Alexander V, who died the following year and was succeeded by John XXIII (not to be confused with the inaugurator of the Second Vatican Council); but since the two deposed popes retained a measure of support the result was to add a third pope rather than to end the schism. A second attempt was made six years later in 1415 at the Council of Constance, which was summoned largely at the instigation of the Holy Roman Emperor Sigismund. John XXIII, the "Pisan" pope, reluctantly went along with summoning the council; but when it became clear that it was unwilling to support his position as he had hoped, and sought rather the resignation or deposition of all three popes, he took fright and flight. On the night of March 20/21, 1415 he fled from Constance, dressed in a disguise variously described as that of a stableboy or of a washer-woman, to nearby Schaffhausen. While he was in exile there, and subsequently at Breisach, issuing various threats against the council, including to dissolve it, the council issued its famous decree on the superiority of the council over the pope. The decree is usually called *Haec sancta*, according to the Latin of the first words ("This holy") after the opening invocation of the Trinity, though it is sometimes known as *Sacrosancta* in accordance with an alternative reading in some manuscripts. The decree reads as follows:

In the name of the holy and undivided Trinity, Father and Son and Holy Spirit. Amen. This holy synod of Constance, which is a general council, for the eradication of the present schism and for bringing unity and reform to God's church in head and members, legitimately assembled in the holy Spirit to the praise of almighty God, ordains, defines, decrees, discerns and declares as follows, in order that this union and reform of God's church may be obtained the more easily, securely, fruitfully and freely.

First it declares that, legitimately assembled in the holy Spirit, constituting a general council and representing the catholic church militant, it has power immediately from Christ; and that everyone of whatever state or dignity, even papal, is bound to obey it in those matters which pertain to the faith, the eradication of the said schism and the general reform of the said church of God in head and members.

Next it declares that anyone of whatever condition, state or dignity, even papal, who contumaciously refuses to obey the past or future mandates, statutes, ordinances or precepts of this sacred council or of any other legitimately assembled general council, regarding the aforesaid things or matters pertaining to them, shall be subjected to well-deserved penance, unless he repents, and shall be duly punished, even by having recourse, if necessary, to other supports of the law. . . . [A-T, p. 409]

Although the decree comes out of a particular situation— the council's wish to establish its authority in the face of John XXIII's threats of disruption—it moves in the second and third paragraphs to the principle of the superiority of any general council over the pope. The areas of this superiority, moreover, are quite wide: "in matters pertaining to the faith, the eradication of the said schism and the general reform of the church of God in head and members."

Eventually the council succeeded in deposing John XXIII and the pope of the Avignon line, Benedict XIII, and in persuading the third claimant, Gregory XII of the Roman or Urbanite line, to resign. At the moment of its triumph it issued two more important decrees, *Frequens* and *Quanto romanus pontifex*, which are also named after the opening words of the decrees. They read as follows:

> The frequent holding of general councils is a pre-eminent means of cultivating the Lord's patrimony. It roots out the briars, thorns and thistles of heresies, errors and schisms, corrects deviations, reforms what is deformed and produces a richly fertile crop for the Lord's vineyard. Neglect of councils, on the other hand, spreads and fosters the afore-said evils. This conclusion is brought before our eyes by the memory of past times and reflection on the present situation.
>
> For this reason we establish, enact, decree and ordain, by a perpetual edict, that general councils shall be held henceforth in the following way. The first shall follow in five years immediately after the end of this council, the second in seven years immediately after the end of the next council, and thereafter they are to be held every ten years for ever. They are to be held in places which the supreme pontiff is bound to nominate and assign within a month before the end of each preceding council, with the approval and consent of the council, or which, in his default, the council itself is bound to nominate. Thus, by a certain continuity, there will always be either a council in existence or one expected within a given time. . . . [A-T, pp. 438–39]

* * *

> Since the Roman pontiff exercises such great power among mortals, it is right that he be bound all the more by the incontrovertible bonds of the faith and by the rites that are to be observed regarding the church's sacraments. We therefore decree and ordain, in order that the fullness of the faith may shine in a future Roman pontiff with singular splendour from the earliest moments of his becoming pope, that henceforth whoever is to be elected Roman pontiff shall make the following confession and profession in public, in front of his electors, before his election is published.

In the name of the holy and undivided Trinity, Father
and Son and holy Spirit. Amen. In the year of our Lord's
nativity one thousand etc., I, . . . , elected pope, with both
heart and mouth confess and profess to almighty God,
whose church I undertake with his assistance to govern,
and to blessed Peter, prince of the apostles, that as long as
I am in this fragile life I will firmly believe and hold the
catholic faith according to the traditions of the apostles, of
the general councils and of other holy fathers, especially the
eight holy universal councils—namely the first at Nicaea,
the second at Constantinople, the third at Ephesus, the
fourth at Chalcedon, the fifth and sixth at Constantinople,
the seventh at Nicaea and the eighth at Constantinople—as
well as of the general councils at the Lateran, Lyons and
Vienne, and I will preserve this faith unchanged to the last
dot and will confirm, defend and preach it to the point of
death and the shedding of my blood, and likewise I will follow and observe in every way the rite handed down of the
ecclesiastical sacraments of the catholic church. This my
profession and confession, written at my orders by a notary
of the holy Roman church, I have signed below with my
own hand. I sincerely offer it on this altar . . . to you,
almighty God, with a pure mind and a devout conscience,
in the presence of the following. [A-T, p. 442]

The decree *Frequens* ruled that another general council
should take place five years immediately after the end of the present one, a second seven years later, and thereafter there was to
be one every ten years for ever. The decree, moreover, established a mechanism for ensuring that the councils took place if
the pope refused to cooperate in summoning them. *Quanto
romanus pontifex* provided an oath that the next pope was
obliged to take, and it gives a good picture of the constitutional
checks on the papacy that the council envisaged.

J. N. Figgis, an English historian, described the decree
Haec sancta as "probably the most revolutionary official document in the history of the world, striving to turn into a tepid

constitutionalism the divine authority of a thousand years. The (conciliar) movement is the culmination of medieval constitutionalism. It forms the watershed between the medieval and the modern world" [2b, Figgis, 1907, p. 31]. This is strong language and in many ways the council saw itself as conservative rather than revolutionary, returning to the balanced and conciliar forms of church government of the early church that had been jeopardized by developments toward papal monarchy and absolutism since the Gregorian reform of the late eleventh century onward.

The council was exhausted by its efforts to heal the schism, having sat for almost three years before it elected the new pope, Martin V, so it had scarcely begun to tackle the reform of the church, its second main purpose, before it decided to dissolve and to postpone reform until the next council.

The importance of Constance lies in the constitutional framework it provided for the church, principally the decrees *Haec sancta, Frequens,* and *Quanto romanus pontifex,* but the status of these three decrees is hotly debated among Roman Catholic scholars. Are they to be considered authentic decrees of an ecumenical or general council? On the one hand, the papacy was uneasy about them inasmuch as they might be interpreted as limiting its authority. When Gregory XII, the Roman or Urbanite pope, resigned in July 1415 he did not confirm the decree *Haec sancta,* which had been promulgated by the council shortly before. Reservations about the decrees were expressed by Martin V and more strongly by Eugenius IV, the popes who followed the ending of the schism. In 1462 Pope Pius II issued the bull *Execrabilis,* which forbade appeals from the pope to a council, though it does not explicitly mention *Haec sancta.* At the time of the Counter-Reformation and later there were various attempts to exclude the Council of Constance from the list of ecumenical or general councils, at least the part of it held before the resignation of Gregory XII and including, therefore, the decree *Haec sancta*: though significantly all the council's decrees were included in the semi-authoritative Roman edition of the councils [above, pp. 7–8 and 49].

There was widespread agreement within western Christendom, however, that Constance was a legitimate council and that it had properly promulgated the three decrees in question. Later, following this consensus, all the churches of the Reformation adopted some form of conciliar government. The papacy, moreover, never rejected the decrees of Constance in an explicit and authoritative manner, and it issued several confirmations of them, albeit sometimes reluctantly. Pope Martin V issued a general confirmation of Constance during the last session of the council [A-T, pp. 450–51, note 4], and various concordats that he reached with secular rulers shortly after the council, as well as others involving Eugenius IV toward the end of Basle-Florence, contained confirmations of Constance and its decrees. Eugenius accepted several reaffirmations of *Haec sancta* and *Frequens* that were made by the Council of Basel [A-T, pp. 457 and 476–77]. In recent years, the decrees of Constance, including *Haec sancta*, *Frequens*, and *Quanto romanus pontifex*, were printed in Professor Alberigo's standard edition of the councils, *Conciliorum oecumenicorum decreta*, as well as in the English version, *Decrees of the ecumenical councils*, both of which have ecclesiastical approval [A-T, p. iv].

In my opinion the Council of Constance should be considered a general council of the western church and its three major decrees be taken as authentic. There remains the problem of how to reconcile them with other statements of the church's magisterium, especially the decrees of Vatican I on the papal office. But it is more correct to leave the various statements alongside each other, in a certain healthy tension, than to seek a consistency that does not exist. If you try to find too much consistency in the tradition of the church, or indeed in the teaching of the councils, you will produce artificiality or inaccuracy. The teaching of Constance is one such area where a good dose of incompleteness remains, perhaps to be worked through by the church at a later time.

In the meanwhile, however, the conciliar movement failed. Following the decree *Frequens*, a council met at Pavia in 1423, five years after the end of Constance, later moving to Siena, but few attended and Pope Martin V showed no enthusiasm for it, with the result that little was accomplished. The next council met at Basel in 1431, and it was soon at loggerheads with Pope Eugenius IV, who had succeeded Martin V shortly before the opening of the council. An uneasy truce was eventually reached which held until 1438, when Eugenius, against the wishes of the majority of participants, transferred the council first to Ferrara and then to Florence. The majority remained at Basel, refused to recognize the Council of Ferrara-Florence, and deposed Eugenius as pope, electing in his place the duke of Savoy who took the name of Felix V: Eugenius and the Council of Ferrara-Florence countered with anathemas against the council at Basel. Eugenius eventually prevailed and the council at Basel, having moved to Lausanne, dissolved itself in 1449.

A major factor in Eugenius's victory was his negotiations with the Greek church over reunion. He managed to persuade the delegation from Constantinople to come to Florence rather than to Basel, and the ensuing agreement about reunion was enshrined in the decree *Laetentur caeli*, which was also published in Greek [A-T, pp. 523–28]. Although the decree proved to be of temporary worth and was fairly soon rejected by the Greek church, it appeared at the time to be a considerable success for Eugenius and his council at Florence. It removed an important motive from the council at Basel and added legitimacy to Eugenius's claims against that council and its pope, Felix V. The council at Basel never recovered thereafter, gradually losing its support within western Christendom.

Because the decree *Laetentur caeli* came to be rejected by

the Greek church, it is of historical rather than of lasting theological or ecclesiological interest. Even so, it is of some note.
The eastern delegation was led by the emperor, John VIII Palae-
ologus, and the patriarch, Joseph of Constantinople, though the
latter died before the signing of the decree. With the Turks
almost at the gates of Constantinople, the emperor was eager for
a settlement with the western church, hoping that aid, military
and otherwise, would follow from it. Pope Eugenius looked for
an agreement to promote his cause against the Council of Basel.
Both sides compromised, the West more so than at any other
time in the Middle Ages. The Greeks accepted the legitimacy of
the *Filioque* clause [above, p. 25] but were not obliged to
include it in their creed. A diversity of practice was accepted
regarding leavened and unleavened bread in the Eucharist. On
purgatory, a compromise formula was reached, "their souls are
cleansed after death by cleansing fires," which kept close to
1 Corinthians 3:15 and avoided any suggestion of a place.
Finally, regarding the papacy, its "full power of tending, ruling
and governing the whole church" was recognized but with the
addition of a clause that could be regarded either as justifying or
as qualifying this primacy, "according to (κατά in the Greek text;
quemadmodum in the Latin) the acts of ecumenical councils and
the sacred canons."

Mark of Ephesus was the only bishop of the eastern delegation who declined to sign the decree of reunion, but others
soon recanted when they returned to Constantinople and found
sentiment to the agreement generally hostile. Events were further overtaken by the capture of Constantinople by the Turks in
1453, which made further contact with the eastern church all
but impossible. In recent years, however, *Laetentur Caeli* has
been the subject of renewed interest in discussions between the
Roman Catholic and Orthodox Churches.

Apparent reunions were also reached at the Council of Florence with the Armenian, Coptic, Syriac, and some other

churches [A-T, pp. 534–59, 567–82, and 586–91]. The agreements, however, which seem to have been dictated to the other churches rather than the result of negotiations, as in the case of *Laetentur Caeli*, were only with small sections of these churches, and the effects for them appear to have been fleeting. The importance of the agreements, rather, was internal to the Roman Catholic Church inasmuch as they contained very full statements of belief to which the Roman Catholic Church subsequently felt itself in large measure bound, in some instances with some unease. For example, the decree of reunion with the Armenian church contained detailed treatments of the seven sacraments, including the statement that "the priesthood is bestowed by the handing over of the chalice with the wine and a paten with bread" (usually referred to as "the handing over of the instruments," *traditio instrumentorum*), a teaching that later was reversed by Pope Pius XII, who ruled in his apostolic constitution *Sacramentum ordinis* issued in 1947 that, for the ordination of a priest, only the laying on of hands and the prayer of ordination by the bishop are necessary [*AAS*, vol. 40, 1948, pp. 6–7]. The decree with the Coptic church contains a strong assertion that salvation is impossible outside the church: "It firmly believes, professes and preaches that all those who are outside the catholic church, not only pagans but also Jews or heretics and schismatics, cannot share in eternal life and will go 'into the everlasting fire which was prepared for the devil and his angels' (Matthew 25:41) unless they are joined to the catholic faith before the end of their lives." And a forceful condemnation of circumcision: "Therefore it strictly orders all who glory in the name of Christian, not to practise circumcision either before or after baptism, since whether or not they place their hope in it, it cannot possibly be observed without loss of eternal salvation." Strong language indeed! The same decree, however, gave support for considering both the Orthodox and Protestant as belonging to the one church with Roman Catholics: "through baptism we become members of Christ and of the body of the church." The subsequent influence of these decrees upon the thought and practice of the Roman Catholic Church, including upon the Council of Trent, has been much greater than is usually recognized.

Lateran V, the last of the councils before the Reformation, was summoned by Pope Julius II mainly in order to preempt the Council of Pisa, which had been called by several cardinals hostile to Julius and supported by the king of France, Louis XII. Pisa justified itself on the grounds of the failure of successive popes to call a general council in accordance with the decree *Frequens* of Constance. Much of the time was consumed with issuing decrees against the Council of Pisa and the so-called Pragmatic Sanction of Bourges, which had been enacted by the French crown and church in 1438 and which is often regarded as the foundation document of Gallicanism (see glossary above, p. x). Lateran V discussed reform of the church but accomplished little. There is an ironic and eerie feel about the council. It ended in March 1517, little more than six months before Martin Luther initiated the Reformation by posting his ninety-five theses on the door of the castle church at Wittenburg, yet there is an extraordinary lack of awareness of the impending storm. The words of the final decree of the council, announcing the closing of the council, are especially disturbing: "Finally, it was reported to us (Pope Leo X) on several occasions, through the cardinals and prelates of the three committees (of the council), that no topics remained for them to discuss and that over several months nothing at all new had been brought before them by anyone" [A-T, pp. 652–53].

CHAPTER THREE

Councils of the Modern Era

Introduction

The three general councils of the modern era are so different from each other that they must be treated separately. More than three centuries intervened between Trent (1545–1563) and Vatican I (1869–1870), almost a century between the latter and Vatican II (1962–1965). Their concerns were correspondingly diverse: Trent was dominated by the challenges of the Protestant Reformation, and it formed a major plank of the Roman Catholic response, usually called the Counter-Reformation. Vatican I came to be dominated by a single issue, papal infallibility. Vatican II became consciously—more so than any other council—a council of its time, the mid-twentieth century. There was not the same continuity of style and content in these councils as in with the first seven ecumenical councils or the general councils of the medieval West.

Nevertheless there are some issues that are common to the three councils. First, there is the question of their status. Like the medieval councils they lacked the participation of the eastern church, and they were also without the presence of the churches of the Reformation. Like the medieval councils, therefore, they lacked the fuller ecumenical character of the first seven councils of the church, and inasmuch as the Protestant churches were not represented as voting members they are best described as general councils of the Roman Catholic Church, rather than as general councils of the western church, as for the medieval councils. Even so, they are of great importance inasmuch as the Roman Catholic Church was the largest single church throughout the period in question, and its claims to be the mainstream church have led many Catholic theologians to consider them as ecumenical councils in the full sense or at least as having an ecumenical character (see above, pp. 47–51).

Another point is that despite the diversity of the three councils, there was a fair amount of cross-referencing between them. Trent had something significant to say on an extremely wide range of issues, and it dominated Roman Catholic theology for almost four centuries in a way that only Chalcedon had managed to do earlier. Its continuing force was taken for granted by Vatican I, which indeed gave it a privileged status among earlier councils [A-T, pp. 803–4 and 806], and the main work of Vatican I may be seen as dealing with the chief item of unfinished business from Trent, namely the church and especially the role of the papacy. Vatican II, although it certainly went beyond Trent and Vatican I, had both councils powerfully in the background of its deliberations: Trent on account of its prevailing influence right into the 1950s; Vatican I because the council had closed prematurely and as a result never finished its intended decree on the church, only completing the section on the papacy, so that other aspects of the church awaited full treatment by Vatican II—in the event receiving rather different treatment from what the participants at Vatican I might have expected!

Finally, the three councils dominated both Roman Catholic thought and the conciliar tradition to an unusual extent. Trent's influence upon Roman Catholic theology for several centuries rendered other councils, both general and local, almost unnecessary. Trent seemed to have said everything, so that local councils were needed only to reiterate Trent, not to take independent initiatives. Vatican I promoted the authority of the papacy in teaching faith and morals, so that any alternative to it, including councils, could seem redundant or a threat to its authority. In the case of Vatican II the situation is more complex and still in the process of definition. Councils have flourished at many levels within the church since Vatican II, which fostered the conciliar approach by its encouragement to dialogue and discussion both within the church and outside it. Several conciliar movements have arisen that have gone beyond Vatican II—for example, within the Dutch church soon after Vatican II and within the Latin-American church beginning at Medellin in 1968—though the councils in question owed much to Vatican II for their inspiration and agenda. Directly and indirectly Vatican II has been the most influential event for the Roman Catholic Church, perhaps for all Christian churches, in the second half of the twentieth century. Its continuing influence in the twenty-first century remains to be seen.

Trent

When Martin Luther clashed with ecclesiastical authority over indulgences, he appealed at first to a general council, promising to submit to its decision if it was summoned; though he soon moved his appeal to the Bible. It was, however, almost thirty years after his initial breach with the Roman church in 1517 that the Council of Trent met, in 1545, by which time the Reformation had spread far and wide and the wounds within the church proved too deep to heal. There were several reasons for the long delay. An important one was fear of a revival of the "conciliar ghost"; fear that if a general council was called it would renew the claims of Constance and Basel to the superiority of a general council over the pope. Another problem was the location. The pope wanted a council in Italy, preferably in or near Rome; Emperor Charles V urged that if the council was to have credibility, especially with the German Lutherans, it must not be seen as controlled by the pope. Eventually Trent was agreed upon, a town that lay within Italy but formed part of a fief of the emperor and therefore was acceptable to him. Most of the meetings were held inside the cathedral church.

The council lasted eighteen years, the meetings concentrated into three periods: 1545–1548, 1551–1552, for part of which time the council moved to Bologna, and 1562–1563. For the early sessions barely two dozen bishops and other clerics, mostly Italians, were present and on several occasions the ability to continue was seriously in doubt. In 1548 the council had to be postponed on account of the threat posed by an advancing Lutheran army, and during the long interval from 1552–1562 the reigning pope, Paul IV, showed himself hostile to its continuance. His successor Pius IV, however, reconvened the council, and during this third and final period there was a good attendance of over two hundred bishops, genuinely representative of the Roman Catholic Church. Despite its often precarious nature, the council produced a remarkable set of decrees responding to most of the issues raised by the Reformation.

The council was bold and direct in its approach. In its first substantial decree it proclaimed the Nicene-Constantinopolitan creed of 381 (with the addition of the *Filioque* clause), thus staking its claim to be in the mainstream of the Christian tradition. Then it confronted two of the most contentious issues in the Reformation debate: the relationship between Scripture and tradition as sources of authority in the church; second, the roles of faith and good works in our justification.

Luther and other Reformation theologians are not mentioned by name in the decrees on authority and justification, but the saying associated with them, s*ola scriptura, sola fides*, is evidently in mind. Trent in general, however, and these decrees in particular, are far from the simplistic rejections of the Reformation that they are sometimes portrayed to be. There was a significant group in the council, whose leaders included the Augustinian friar Girolamo Seripando, Cardinal Giovanni Morone, and the English cardinal, Reginald Pole, who wished for what they regarded as the better elements of the Reformation to be taken into consideration; and their views were well represented in the decrees, especially in the early stages of the council.

The decree on authority in the church, "Acceptance of the sacred books and apostolic traditions," reads as follows:

> The holy ecumenical and general Council of Trent, lawfully assembled in the Holy Spirit, with the same three legates of the apostolic see presiding, keeps ever before its eyes this purpose: that the purity of the gospel, purged of all errors, may be preserved in the church. Our Lord Jesus Christ, the Son of God, first proclaimed with his own lips this gospel, which had in the past been promised by the prophets in the sacred scriptures; then he bade it be preached to every creature through his apostles as the source of the whole truth of salvation and rule of conduct. The council clearly perceives that this truth and rule are contained in written books and in unwritten traditions which were received by the apostles from the mouth of Christ himself, or else have come down to us, handed on as it were from the apostles themselves at the inspiration of the holy Spirit. Following the example of the orthodox fathers, the council accepts and venerates with a like feeling of piety and reverence all the books of both the old and the new Testament, since the one God is the author of both, as well as the traditions concerning both faith and conduct, as either directly spoken by Christ or dictated by the holy Spirit, which have been preserved in unbroken sequence in the catholic church. . . .
> [A-T, p. 663]

The decree is scriptural and Christ-centered in its initial approach: to preserve "the purity of the gospel," which "our Lord Jesus Christ . . . first proclaimed with his own lips." In the transmission of the gospel two sources are distinguished, Scripture and tradition, "written books and unwritten traditions." The decree has been criticized for making tradition, and the church as the interpreter of tradition, too independent of Scripture: Vatican II, in its decree on Revelation, sought to link the two together more closely [below pp. 106–7]. There is some truth in the criticism but it should not be accepted too easily, for the decree emphasizes that the two sources are joined by their common origin, the good news proclaimed by Jesus Christ.

The decree on justification and that on original sin which goes with it enter into serious debate with the Reformers. In reply to their emphasis on the depravity of human nature, the council states that the guilt of original sin is truly remitted through Baptism, not just "erased and not attributed," but "concupiscence or a tendency to sin remains" [A-T, p. 667]. On justification the decree, in chapter 5, goes along with the Reformers' insistence that all the initiative comes from God, "from a predisposing grace of God through Jesus Christ," but we have a role in "giving free assent to and cooperating with this same grace."

> [A]ctual justification in adults takes its origin from a predisposing grace of God through Jesus Christ, that is, from his invitation which calls them, with no existing merits on their side; thus, those who had been turned away from God by sins are disposed by God's grace inciting and helping them, to turn towards their own justification by giving free assent to and co-operating with this same grace. Consequently, though God touches a person's heart through the light of the holy Spirit, neither does that person do absolutely nothing in receiving that movement of grace, for he can also reject it; nor is he able, by his own free will and without God's grace, to move himself towards justice in God's sight. Hence when scripture says, "Return to me and I will return to you" [Zechariah 1:3], we are reminded of our freedom; when we answer, "Restore us to yourself, O Lord, that we may be restored" [Lamentations 5:21], we

are admitting that we are forestalled by the grace of God. [A-T, p. 672]

In chapter 10 the decree gives a beautiful description of how we can grow in holiness.

So those justified in this way and made friends and members of the household of God, going from strength to strength, are, as the Apostle says, renewed from day to day by putting to death what is earthly in themselves [Colossians 3:5] and yielding themselves as instruments of righteousness for sanctification [Romans 6:13 and 19] by observance of the commandments of God and of the church. They grow and increase in that very justness they have received through the grace of Christ, by faith united to good works, as it is written: "Let him who is holy become more holy" [Apocalypse 22:11]; and again, "Do not wait until death to be justified" [Ecclesiasticus 18:22]; again, "you see that a person is justified by works and not by faith alone" [James 2:24]. Indeed, holy church asks for this increase in justice when it prays, "Lord, give us an increase in faith, hope and charity" [Prayer of thirteenth Sunday after Pentecost]. [A-T, p. 675]

Many other topics in the Reformation debate hinged on the two questions of the relationship between Scripture and tradition and that between faith and good works. Trent issued a wide range of decrees on these topics, seeking to justify teaching and practices that had become traditional in the church and to show their roots in Scripture and the early church, while at the same time purifying both teaching and practice of abuses.

The sacraments were treated at length. There was a decree on the sacraments in general, defending the seven sacraments of Baptism, confirmation, penance or confession, Eucharist, last anointing, marriage, and orders, which had become the traditional teaching by the thirteenth century, against the doctrine of two sacraments, Baptism and Eucharist, which was common

among the Reformers; and one or more decrees on each of the
sacraments in particular.

The Eucharist was treated in great detail, for although it
was acknowledged as a sacrament by the Reformers, there were
fierce disputes about its nature both between Catholics and
Reformers and among different groups of the latter. The treatment of the Eucharist contains much of beauty, devotion, and
careful theology; though the doctrine of transubstantiation,
enunciated briefly at the Fourth Lateran Council of 1215, as we
have seen [above, p. 56], but now stated in a harder form,
proved to be a major stumbling-block for all Reformers:

> If anyone says that . . . the substance of bread and wine
> remains together with the body and blood of our Lord
> Jesus Christ, and denies that marvellous and unique change
> of the whole substance of the bread into the body, and of
> the whole substance of the wine into the blood, while only
> the appearance (Latin, *species*) of bread and wine remains, a
> change which the catholic church most aptly calls transub-
> stantiation, let him be anathema. [A-T, p. 697; see also
> p. 695]

The decree dates from the second period of the council,
1551–1552, by which time there had occurred a certain hard-
ening toward the Reformers, and this change continued into the
third period from 1562–1563.

It is interesting to note, however, that the council issued
three separate invitations to Protestants to attend [A-T, pp. 702,
719–21, and 724–25]. Two were addressed to the German
Protestants, in 1551 and 1552, and the third in 1562 extended
to "each and all who are not in communion with us in matters
of faith, from whatever kingdoms, nations, provinces, cities and
places they come." The conditions were generous: a safe conduct to and from the council and freedom there "to propose and
offer in writing or in speech as many points as they shall choose

. . . and to hold debate without any violent abuse or invective." Some Protestants considered accepting the invitation, but they wanted the council to start again from the beginning, putting aside the decrees that had already been passed. This proved a sticking point, so that very few Protestants came, and there were no serious debates. Still, the invitations are indicative of a measure of openness on the part of the council.

Other doctrinal topics in debate with Protestants received decrees, mostly toward the end of the council: purgatory, the intercession of saints, indulgences. Ironically, the decree on indulgences, the immediate occasion of the Reformation, was passed only at the very last session of the council.

At an early date the council had defined its aims as "the rooting out of heresy and the reform of conduct" [A-T, p. 662]. The second aim, the reform of conduct, was pursued alongside the decrees of a more doctrinal nature—there was of course a fair amount of overlap between doctrine and conduct—and the results were extensive though on the whole less complete than in the area of doctrine. Instruction and preaching; the suitability and responsibilities of persons appointed to benefices, including the abuses of pluralism and nonresidence; religious orders of men and women; various devotional practices, including devotions to saints and fasting: these were all treated at some length, though in some cases with too much allowance for papal and other dispensations, too much concern for vested interests, to satisfy the wishes of more thoroughgoing Catholic reformers.

In addition, there was a decree on seminaries, which proved to be very influential. Until that time the training of most diocesan priests was relatively unorganized. A few studied at a university, but for the others an informal apprenticeship, partly with the local parish priest, was the norm. Trent's decree ordered the establishment of diocesan colleges for boys of twelve years old and upward, with preference being given to the sons of the poor, who would be given a mixture of spiritual, academic, and practical training. It is a long decree, much of which is taken up with the financial arrangements of the seminaries, but the aims are stated at the beginning and the passage gives a good insight into the pastoral approach of the council.

> If they are not rightly brought up, those of adolescent years tend to make for the world's pleasures and, unless trained to religious practice from an early age before habits of vice take firm hold on so many, they never keep to an orderly church life in an exemplary way without great and almost extraordinary help from almighty God.
>
> Hence the holy council decrees that every cathedral, metropolitan and greater church is obliged to provide for, to educate in religion and to train in ecclesiastical studies a set number of boys, according to its resources and the size of the diocese. The boys are to be drawn from the city and diocese, or its province if the former do not provide sufficient, and educated in a college chosen for the purpose by the bishop near to these churches or in another convenient place. Those admitted to the college should be at least twelve years old, of legitimate birth, who know how to read and write competently, and whose character and disposition offers hope that they will serve in church ministries throughout life. The council wishes the sons of poor people particularly to be chosen, but does not exclude those of the more wealthy provided they pay for their own maintenance and show an ambition to serve God and the church.
>
> The bishop will divide these boys into the number of classes he thinks fit, according to their number, age and progress in ecclesiastical learning. Some he will assign to service of the churches when he considers the time is ripe, others he will keep for education in the college: he will replace those withdrawn with others, so that the college becomes a perpetual seminary of ministers of God. So that they may be more appropriately grounded in ecclesiastical studies, they should always have the tonsure and wear clerical dress from the outset; they should study grammar, singing, keeping church accounts and other useful skills; and they should be versed in holy scripture, church writers,

homilies of the saints, and the practice of rites and cere-
monies and of administering the sacraments, particularly all
that seems appropriate to hearing confessions. The bishop
should ensure that they attend mass every day, confess their
sins at least every month, receive the body of our Lord
Jesus Christ as often as their confessor judges, and serve in
the cathedral and other churches of the area on feast days.

In consultation with two of the senior and more experi-
enced canons of their choosing, bishops are to see to all
these arrangements and any others useful or necessary for
this enterprise, as the holy Spirit may prompt, and by con-
stant visitation ensure that they are always kept in force.
They will punish the difficult and incorrigible and those
who spread bad habits with severity, and expel them if need
be; and they will take the utmost care to remove all obstacles from such a worthy and holy foundation and promote
all that preserves and strengthens it. . . . [A-T, pp. 750–51]

In some regions seminaries were established quickly, for
example in the areas under the authority of Charles Borromeo,
archbishop of Milan, but elsewhere the process was much
slower. Eventually, however, the decree had a revolutionary
effect on the training of priests in the Roman Catholic Church,
mostly for the better. A criticism is that it removed candidates
for the priesthood too soon from the mainstream of life, accen-
tuating the separation of a priestly caste. It is noticeable that in
recent years, especially following Vatican II's decree on the formation of priests, there has been renewed emphasis on future
priests keeping in contact with "ordinary life," through work
and other assignments in parishes during their training: in a
sense, a return to the medieval arrangements.

The council at its last session entrusted the pope with the
task of the drawing up of a list of "books that were suspect or
dangerous," the publication of a catechism, and revisions of the
missal and breviary. These measures resulted in a revised
"Index" of books that Catholics were forbidden to read, the

"Catechism of Trent," the Roman Missal, containing the rite that later came to be known as the "Tridentine Mass," and the Roman breviary: all of which had profound effects on the life and thinking of Roman Catholics for several centuries.

Indeed, it is hard to exaggerate the influence of the Council of Trent on the Roman Catholic Church in the following four centuries, difficult though this influence is to measure. A few major topics were not accorded decrees by the council, but usually this was wise because they concerned subjects on which there was insufficient consensus among Roman Catholics, so that on the whole the council did not go beyond what members of the church could agree to. There were, for example, no decrees on the nature of the church or on the papacy, for although the topics were hotly debated between Catholics and Reformers, Catholics themselves were divided in their views between conciliarists and papalists. Grace, too, was not treated properly because of theological differences among Catholics, notably between Dominicans and Jesuits.

With these and a few other exceptions, however, the council covered a remarkably wide range of topics with carefully thought-out decrees. We take so many of the decrees for granted, forming as they did a background to Catholic theology for so long, that we easily forget what a striking achievement they are. They are rooted in medieval theology, indeed, yet they form a remarkable clarification and systematization of that theology. The council gave to Roman Catholicism a platform and a confidence, ending the years of defensiveness in the face of the Reformation.

Did the council increase the already existing divisions between Catholics and Reformers? On the one hand, the council to some extent accepted the theology of the Reformation and was open to the Reformer. On the other hand, the council became increasingly anti-Protestant in its later stages, and it became a principal instrument of the more aggressive Catholicism of the Counter-Reformation. By the time the council met in 1545, the wounds resulting from the Reformation were probably too deep to heal. What might have happened if a general council had been called twenty years earlier is a fascinating but hypothetical question. As it is, the council made points that needed to be stated and it may be seen as the best that could be done by the Roman Catholic Church in the circumstances.

The council was influential primarily within the Roman Catholic Church. However, inasmuch as the churches of the Reformation had to take into account the renewed Catholic Church that resulted from it, its influence was much wider: indeed it profoundly affected European civilization and, through it, the wider world. Although the council in a sense deepened and prolonged the Reformation divisions, it preserved important points in the Christian tradition and will, hopefully, benefit and enrich reunion between the churches in the end.

Vatican I

The First Vatican Council came as a surprise. Trent still seemed to provide an adequate exposition of Roman Catholic theology, and little need was felt to go beyond its formulations, especially in the debates with the Protestant churches that still dominated apologetics. Another council seemed unnecessary.

Much, however, had been occurring at other levels. The French revolution of 1789 and its aftermath, as well as the industrial revolution beginning in the late eighteenth century, brought huge changes to the political, social, and economic climate of the western world. The Enlightenment, in the eighteenth century, posed many intellectual challenges to Christianity, and these were compounded in the next century by advances in science, which, like Darwin's investigations into the origins of humankind, gave rise to further questions.

As is so often the case in the history of the church, two tendencies can be discerned in the responses to these challenges. On the one hand, there was a more liberal tendency, which accepted what was good in these developments and wanted to see how far Christianity could be reconciled with and enriched by them. On the other hand, there was a more conservative approach that was suspicious of changes, especially those from outside the church, and indeed often opposed them, emphasizing the church's need to proclaim its own message clearly and unequivocally.

It is customary to see Vatican I almost entirely in terms of a victory for the conservatives, but this is an oversimplification. Pope Pius IX, who called the council, was eager that it speak clearly about the the authority of the church, especially the role of the papacy and its infallibility. Elected pope in 1847, he initially had the reputation of a liberal but soon, following his loss of the papal states to the forces of Italian reunification, moved decidedly in a conservative direction. In 1864 he issued a Syllabus of Errors, which contained a widespread attack on recent developments and ended with a condemnation of all who said that "the Roman pontiff can and ought to reconcile and adjust himself with progress, liberalism and modern civilization" [D-H, no. 2980]. Even so, the first of the two decrees promulgated by the council represented a serious attempt to dialogue with the intellectual world of the time. Indeed, one might go as far as to say that this was the first time, at least since the early church, that an ecumenical or general council had directly addressed the wider intellectual world beyond the Christian community.

The first decree, "Constitution on the Catholic Faith" (Latin title, *Dei Filius*), contained four chapters entitled "God the Creator of All Things," "Revelation," "Faith," "Faith and reason." The fourth and last chapter dealt most explicitly with the intellectual challenges of the day, seeking to steer a middle course between an excessive exaltation of the authority of reason, exemplified by much of the Enlightenment, on the one hand, and a rejection of reason, often characteristic of religious fundamentalism and in part of the Romantic movement, on the other hand:

> The perpetual agreement of the catholic church has maintained and maintains this too: that there is a twofold order of knowledge, distinct not only as regards its source but also as regards its object. With regard to its source, we know at the one level by natural reason, at the other by divine faith. With regard to the object, besides those things to which natural reason can attain, there are proposed for our belief mysteries hidden in God which, unless they are divinely revealed, are incapable of being known. . . .
>
> Even though faith is above reason, there can never be any real disagreement between faith and reason, since it is the same God who reveals the mysteries and infuses faith, and who has endowed the human mind with the light of reason. . . . Not only can faith and reason never be at odds with one another but they mutually support each other, for on the one hand right reason established the foundations of the faith and, illuminated by its light, develops the science of divine things; on the other hand, faith delivers reason from errors and protects it and furnishes it with knowledge of many kinds. Hence, so far is the church from hindering the development of human arts and studies, that in fact she assists and promotes them in many ways. For she is neither ignorant nor contemptuous of the advantages which derive from this source of human life, rather she acknowledges that those things flow from God, the lord of sciences, and, if they are properly used, lead to God by the help of his grace. Nor does the church forbid these studies to employ, each within its own area, its own proper principles and method: but while she admits this just freedom, she takes particular care that they do not become infected with errors by conflicting with divine teaching, or, by going beyond their proper limits, intrude upon what belongs to faith and engender confusion. . . . [A-T, pp. 808–9]

For some people the approach was too dualist and two-tiered, leading to a sharp distinction between faith and reason, nature and the supernatural, with too much authority being accorded to faith and the church. Certainly the decree left areas for theologians to work on during the following century, yet it shows a positive appreciation of human creativity and the advancement of science.

Vatican I is chiefly known for its second decree, "Constitution on the Church of Christ" (Latin title, *Pastor aeternus*), especially the chapter on papal infallibility. The original intention had been to produce a full decree on the church, thus filling the gap left by Trent. The threat of the withdrawal of the French and German bishops from the council, owing to the impending Franco-Prussian war, and that posed by the Italian troops under Garibaldi, now almost at the gates of Rome, introduced urgency into the situation. As a result, on the initiative of the pope, the council agreed to discuss first the part of the decree concerning the papacy. This part developed into a decree in itself and was all that the council managed to treat.

Parts of the decree are acceptable both to Catholics and Orthodox and even to some Protestants: that a certain primacy among the apostles and over the church had been given to Peter and that, inasmuch as Christ wished his church to continue, this primacy remains with the popes down to the present, as successors of Peter, the bishop of Rome. The nature of this primacy, however, was defined in terms that are unacceptable both to the Orthodox and Reformed churches and have proved difficult for many Catholics. In particular, the teaching that the pope has "the full and supreme power of jurisdiction over the whole church, not only in matters of faith and morals, but also in those which concern the discipline and government of the church dispersed throughout the whole world, . . . an absolute fullness of this supreme power . . . that . . . is ordinary and immediate both over all and each of the churches and over all and each of the pastors and faithful" [A-T, pp. 814–15] clashed with the Orthodox concept of the autonomy of individual churches in the ordinary conduct of their affairs and was anathema to the ecclesiology of the churches of the Reformation. Some Catholics, too, feared that the teaching diluted the authority of bishops and made them little more than delegates of the pope, but the decree also stated: "This power of the supreme pontiff by no means detracts from that ordinary and immediate power of episcopal jurisdiction, by which bishops, who have succeeded to the place of the apostles by appointment of the holy Spirit, tend and govern individually the particular flocks which have been assigned to them. On the contrary, this power of theirs is asserted, supported and defended by the supreme and universal pastor" [A-T, p. 814].

The primacy of the pope included an "infallible teaching authority," the decree stated. The crucial passage reads as follows:

> Therefore, faithfully adhering to the tradition received from the beginning of the Christian faith, to the glory of God our saviour, for the exaltation of the catholic religion and for the salvation of the Christian people, with the approval of the sacred council, we teach and define as a divinely revealed dogma that when the Roman pontiff speaks *ex cathedra*, that is, when, in the exercise of his office as shepherd and teacher of all Christians, in virtue of his supreme apostolic authority, he defines a doctrine concerning faith or morals to be held by the whole church, he possesses, by the divine assistance promised to him in blessed Peter, that infallibility which the divine Redeemer willed his church to enjoy in defining doctrine concerning faith or morals. Therefore, such definitions of the Roman pontiff are of themselves, and not by the consent of the church, irreformable.
>
> So then, should anyone, which God forbid, have the temerity to reject this definition of ours: let him be anathema. [A-T, p. 816]

Several points should be noted. First, the pope's infallibility is set within definite boundaries. He must be speaking in solemn form, *ex cathedra*, so that casual remarks to journalists or to friends at a dinner, for example, would not fulfill the conditions. He must, too, be defining a doctrine about "faith or morals," so that the pope cannot rely on infallibility in, for example, predicting the weather or the outcome of a football game. The Latin original for "morals," *mores*, is difficult to translate; it has somewhat wider connotations than "morals" as usually understood, partly including customs and behavior and therefore church order; some writers prefer to translate it simply as "practice." The matter to be defined must be one that is "to be held by the whole church," which is sometimes glossed as meaning—though the text does not strictly speaking say so—that the issue must be of major importance or central to the faith; at any rate, it excludes matters that pertain only to particular regions or groups of people, for example, the justice or injustice of a particular war.

Second, the text does not say directly that the pope is infallible. It says, rather, that when the above-mentioned conditions have been fulfilled, the pope "possesses . . . the infallibility which the divine Redeemer willed his church to enjoy." In other words, the pope's infallibility is placed within the context of the church's, not outside it. What is meant by the church is not stated, but it is reasonable to think of it not just in terms of the hierarchical church but also, indeed primarily, as the people of God, the Christian faithful, as indicated later in Vatican II's decree on the church, *Lumen gentium*. The pope, therefore, shares in the guidance promised to the whole Christian people: though the passage warns against an overreductionist approach, ending: "Therefore, such definitions of the Roman pontiff are of themselves, and not by consent of the church, irreformable."

Also, infallibility is given to the pope "to the glory of God our saviour, for the exaltation of the catholic religion and for the salvation of the Christian people." In other words, it is given for an ulterior purpose, especially the service of the church, not for the personal gratification of the pope.

The decree, nevertheless, raises a number of questions. There is the problem that despite the criteria given in the decree, it is difficult to say which definitions should be considered infallible. Some minimalists have argued that only three definitions fulfill the conditions: the definition of infallibility itself and those about Mary's immaculate conception, in 1854, and her assumption, in 1950. Others extend the net much wider. It is clear, however, that the church has never issued a list of infallible teachings. "No doctrine is understood to be infallibly defined unless this is manifestly demonstrated," states the 1983 Code of Canon Law (Roman Catholic Church), canon 749. Another argument is that the definition introduced an unhealthy distinction between infallible and noninfallible doctrines, as if the latter can readily be challenged. Before Vatican I, the argument goes, there was a more nuanced and healthier grading in the status of doctrines, shading gradually and according to a variety of criteria from less to more authoritative ones. There is some truth in the argument, though Vatican I certainly never intended to downgrade noninfallible teachings.

Another point is that the degree of infallibility is left unexplained. On the one hand the decree, in an earlier passage, asserts confidently that "in the apostolic see the catholic religion has always been preserved unblemished." On the other hand, opponents of the definition at the council pointed to errors made by popes in the past. The condemnations of Pope Honorius, mentioned earlier [above, pp. 34–35], the judgment on the astronomer Galileo in the seventeenth century, and some other cases were well known; one might well add today the steadfast encouragement given by popes to the crusades and the Inquisition and their often ambivalent attitude to the Jews. As a result, either one has to argue that these cases do not fulfill the conditions laid down by Vatican I for infallibility, for example, that the judgments were not made sufficiently solemnly or *ex cathedra*. Or that infallibility guarantees a general guidance, such as is given to the church as a whole, but does not extend to all particular details. Both approaches provide some awkwardness.

Finally, there is the question of pressure and lack of unanimity. The points were made forcibly by A. B. Hasler, who argued that the pressure put upon members of the council by Pope Pius and the size of the opposition to the definition of infallibility cast serious doubts upon the decree's validity [2d, Hasler, 1981]. It is true that Pius took a personal interest in the decree and urged members of the council to vote for it, in some cases in strong terms. Many criticized, with some justification, the ways in which procedures at the council were manipulated to favor the passing of the decree. There were various pressures and a fair amount of politicking, some rather devious. On the other hand, the opponents of the definition were able to look after themselves and their cause, the final vote was free, and there had been at least as much pressure at several previous councils, at Ephesus in 431, for example. It is difficult to argue that the pressure was sufficient to invalidate the decree unless you rule out much else in the church's history!

Regarding unanimity, certainly it was recognized that a general consensus was desirable, not just a simple majority; though the need for unanimity, or virtual unanimity, had never been stated clearly and authoritatively. Opposition to the definition among members of the council was significant, though opponents gave various reasons for their opposition, from those opposed to it in principle to the more numerous so-called inopportunists, who, while not necessarily opposed to the definition in principle, thought nevertheless that it was unwise or inopportune for various reasons—its likely discouraging effects on relations with other Christian churches, for example. The opponents included many prominent prelates: almost the entire Austro-

Hungarian episcopate under the leadership of Cardinal Rauscher; most German bishops; a considerable number of French prelates, including the archbishops of Paris and Lyons; several North American archbishops; the archbishop of Milan; and three eastern patriarchs; as well as many clergy and laity who were not members of the council, notably the scholars Johann von Döllinger and Lord Acton and the former Anglican priest John Henry Newman. According to some calculations, the bishops of the minority represented, in terms of the populations of their (in many cases, large) dioceses, over half the worldwide Catholic population. It is essential, however, to appreciate the strong sentiments in favor of the definition.

At a preliminary vote on the draft decree on July 13, 1870, 451 voted yes (*placet*), 88 no (*non-placet*), and 62 had reservations (*placet iuxta modum*). Before the final vote, which took place five days later, some sixty or more bishops (estimates of the number vary) left Rome, most of them, it seems clear, preferring this form of abstention to voting openly against the decree. The final vote was 533 in favor and only two against (the bishops of Little Rock, Arkansas, U.S.A, and Caiazzo in southern Italy).

On July 19, the day after the promulgation of the decree, war broke out between France and Prussia, resulting in the departure from the council of most remaining bishops of these two countries and the withdrawal from Rome of the French troops who had been defending the city for the pope against the Italian forces. Some work continued to be done during the summer; but on September 20 Garibaldi's troops entered Rome, and the council was terminated. A month later Pius formally adjourned the proceedings indefinitely.

Altogether some seven hundred bishops attended the council, roughly two-thirds of those eligible. They came from all five continents, and in this sense it was the most ecumenical council ever, though the overwhelming majority were Europeans, either with sees in Europe or in terms of their ethnic ori-

gins: 35 percent were Italians (there were many small sees in
southern Italy, and many Italian prelates in the Roman curia)
and 17 percent were French (there were many French missionary bishops), amounting to over half the total. About sixty were
bishops of churches of eastern rites in communion with Rome.
The Orthodox and Protestant churches were not represented.

Vatican I, dominated by the definition of papal infallibility,
is undoubtedly a controversial council both within the Catholic
Church and in its relations with other churches and the wider
world. It made claims that many find impossible to accept and
that may appear to show the Catholic Church at its most aggressive and authoritarian. When the definition of infallibility is read
carefully, however, it appears much less threatening and alarmist,
perhaps indeed a reassuring statement of God's promise to stay
close to and guide the church, in which the bishop of Rome has
a special place. Various points expressed by the opponents of the
definition were incorporated into the decree so that the final text
proved acceptable, in the end and albeit only grudgingly in a fair
number of cases, to all the bishops. The theology is skewed in
favor of the papacy and so required complementing by consideration of other members of the church: it is providential that
almost a century of further reflection elapsed before this work
was accomplished at Vatican II.

Vatican II

Vatican II is a remarkable council. In recent years I have had the
privilege of giving many lectures on the councils of the church,
and Vatican II appears ever more extraordinary. Indeed, for all
the problems in the church today, which at times seem formida-
ble, we are are nevertheless the most fortunate Christians ever
because we are the only generation to have lived in the light of
this great council. The older among us are especially fortunate

because to have lived before the council as well as after it adds greatly to the appreciation!

Vatican II, like Vatican I, came unexpectedly. The theology of Trent still exercised great influence in the 1950s, and Vatican I's definition of papal infallibility seemed to provide a means for solving any future debates. Papal infallibility had been used, apparently successfully, by Pope Pius XII in 1950, in the proclamation of Mary's assumption into heaven. Another general council seemed to many people unnecessary.

When, therefore, Pope John XXIII announced on January 25, 1959, three months after his election, that he wished to convoke a new ecumenical council, there was considerable surprise. Though it is true that both Pius XI (1922–1939) and Pius XII (1939–1958) had spoken at various times of summoning a council to complete the work of Vatican I. There is much debate among scholars as to how far Pope John knew what he was doing, to what extent he had a conscious plan. The indications are somewhat conflicting. He spoke of wishing to open the windows of the church in order to let in fresh air; he also said that the purpose of the council was to strengthen doctrine and improve ecclesiastical discipline, proposals that are open to varying interpretations. Other moves, such as his confirmation of the strict decrees concerning the clergy that were issued by the synod of the diocese of Rome in January 1960, which John XXIII had summoned, or his re-imposition of Latin as the language of teaching in seminaries, appear conservative. In the letter *Humanae salutis* of December 1961, in which the pope officially summoned the council to meet the following year, three main aims were given: the better internal ordering of the church, unity among Christians, and the promotion of peace throughout the world. John was a shrewd man and deeply spiritual; attention to the Holy Spirit, wherever she might blow, seemed to dominate his actions; he also had a good sense of history, being himself a historian of some note. The council met for about ten weeks in the autumn of each of the four years 1962–1965; John XXIII died in June 1963, and Paul VI succeeded him as pope a few weeks later.

What seems clear is that nobody, including Pope John, foresaw how the council would develop. Before the council the Roman curia had been allowed to prepare draft documents, but these quickly proved unacceptable to the council, so new decrees had to be hammered out almost from scratch. Some idea of the long development that resulted is given by the dates on which the council eventually approved its sixteen decrees. The titles and dates of the decrees are as follows, with the chapter headings of some of them added: in subsequent quotations, reference is made to the official "numbers" into which the decrees are divided and the translations are taken from the *Decrees* volumes in A-T.

* * *

1. Constitution on the Sacred Liturgy, *Sacrosanctum concilium* (December 4, 1963)
2. Decree on the Mass Media, *Inter mirifica* (December 4, 1963)
3. Dogmatic Constitution on the Church, *Lumen gentium* (November 21, 1964)
   chap. 1. The Mystery of the Church
   chap. 2. The People of God
   chap. 3. The Hierarchical Constitution of the Church and in Particular the Episcopate
   chap. 4. The Laity
   chap. 5. The Universal Call to Holiness in the Church
   chap. 6. Religious
   chap. 7. The Eschatological Character of the Pilgrim Church and Its Union with the Heavenly Church

chap. 8. The Blessed Virgin Mary, Mother of God, in the Mystery of Christ and the Church
  I. Introduction
  II. The Role of the Blessed Virgin in the Economy of Salvation
  III. The Blessed Virgin and the Church
  IV. The Cult of the Blessed Virgin in the Church
  V. Mary, the Sign of Sure Hope and Comfort for the Pilgrim People of God. Clarifications

4. Decree on the Eastern Catholic Churches, *Orientalium ecclesiarum* (November 21, 1964)

5. Decree on Ecumenism, *Unitatis redintegratio* (November 21, 1964)

6. Decree on the Pastoral Office of Bishops in the Church, *Christus Dominus* (October 28, 1965)

7. Decree on the Sensitive Renewal of Religious Life, *Perfectae caritatis* (October 28, 1965)

8. Decree on Priestly Formation, *Optatam totius* (October 28, 1965)

9. Declaration of Christian Education, *Gravissimum educationis* (October 28, 1965)

10. Declaration on the Church's Relation to Non-Christian Religions, *Nostra aetate* (October 28, 1965)

11. Dogmatic Constitution on Divine Revelation, *Dei verbum* (November 18, 1965)

12. Decree on the Apostolate of the Laity, *Apostolicam actuositatem* (November 18, 1965)

13. Declaration on Religious Freedom, *Dignitatis humanae* (December 7, 1965)

14. Decree on the Missionary Activity of the Church, *Ad gentes* (December 7, 1965)

15. Decree on the Ministry and Life of Priests, *Presbyterorum ordinis* (December 7, 1965)

16. Pastoral Constitution on the Church in the World of Today, *Gaudium et spes* (December 7, 1965)

It was, therefore, only toward the end of the second year
of the council, on December 4, 1963, that the first two decrees
were passed, on liturgy and the mass media. An important reason for the relatively early acceptance of the decree on the liturgy
was that it provided common ground between the conservative
and progressive or liberal groupings within the council—ironically so inasmuch as the decree proved to be, in its implementa-

tion after the council, perhaps the most contentious of all the decrees. There was general agreement among the different parties on two points: the need for greater participation in the liturgy, especially on the part of the laity and in the Eucharist, and, second, the need to return to the sources of the liturgy. Pope Pius XII had issued a major document on the reform of the liturgy in 1947, the encyclical letter *Mediator Dei*, and later he instituted an imaginative reform of the liturgy of Holy Week and Easter. Many scholars, notably Benedictine monks, had worked on improving understanding of the liturgy of the early church. Thus, the decree promulgated was very much the fruit of various initiatives in the years before the council.

Regarding the principle of participation the decree is clear: "The church very much wants all believers to be led to take a full, conscious and active participation in liturgical celebration. This is demanded by the nature of the liturgy itself: and, by virtue of their baptism, it is the right and the duty of the Christian people." Regarding the means to this participation, however, the decree is much more cautious. Thus, on the change from Latin to the vernacular languages, which proved to be perhaps the most momentous change of all, the decree, far from simply pushing it through, says rather, "The use of the Latin language is to be maintained in the Latin rites." Immediately, however, it leaves a loophole, "except where a particular law might indicate otherwise." The door is then opened further: "in the mass, the administration of the sacraments and in other parts of the liturgy, there can not at all infrequently (note the double negative—Latin *haud raro*—beloved of Vatican documents, allowing scope for different emphases) exist a practice of using the local language, a practice which is really helpful among the people. It should therefore be possible for more scope to be given for such practices, firstly in the readings and in instructions given to the people, in some prayers and in some of the singing . . ." [no. 36].

Two other emphases may be noted in the decree: first, some delegation of authority to bishops and others in making decisions about the liturgy, and, second, encouragement for the gifts and customs of different groups of people. Indeed, the decree has a section entitled "Norms aimed at bringing about adaptation to the temperament and traditions of peoples," which contains quite strong statements: "In matters that do not affect the faith or the well-being of the whole community, the church has no desire, not even in the liturgy, to impose a rigid monolithic structure. Rather, on the contrary, it cultivates and encourages the gifts and endowments of mind and heart possessed by various races and peoples" [no. 37]. These points would be followed up in other decrees.

The other decree approved at the same time concerned the mass media. It is a short document of no great originality, and it need not detain us long. Even so, its generally positive attitude toward the world of newspapers, cinema, radio, television, and other means of communication is noticeable. It has obvious links with Pius XII's encyclical on the mass media entitled *Miranda prorsus* (the first two words of the encyclical, which translate "Very remarkable," though many Catholics initially thought that Miranda Prorsus was an Italian film star!) published in 1957. The generally optimistic tone of the Vatican II decree and its appreciation of human endeavor and creativity, including outside the Christian community, were to be features of other decrees.

The next three decrees were passed only toward the end of the third year of the council: on the church, the Eastern Catholic churches, and ecumenism, all on November 21, 1964. A decree on the church had been carefully drafted before the council by one of the preparatory commissions, which was headed by the conservative Cardinal Ottaviani, Prefect of the Holy Office, the congregation of the Curia responsible for doctrine. Many had expected it to be the centerpiece of the council's work, completing the unfinished decree of Vatican I on the church. Indeed,

Vatican I had never been formally closed, only prorogued, and the question remained as to whether Vatican II would be deemed a continuation of Vatican I or a separate new council. Pope John XXIII resolved the latter question by declaring Vatican II to be a new council, and the preparatory commission's draft decree on the church was rejected soon after the opening of the council.

The extent of the changes in the decree on the church that eventually emerged is indicated by the headings of its chapters, which are given above. Instead of beginning with the pope and working downward, the approach is humbler and more "from below." The church is defined primarily as a mystery and as the people of God, in the first two chapters. The hierarchical church of pope and bishops is there, in chapter 3, but it comes after the first two chapters and in service of the Christian community. Immediately afterward the decree returns to the wider concept of the church, with chapters on the laity and the call of all Christians to holiness, scotching any suggestion that laypeople are second-class citizens in the church. Religious orders are placed firmly within the church in chapter 6. Chapter 7, on "the eschatological character of the pilgrim church," functions as a summary of the decree so far, and it returns to the theme of chapter 1, the church as a mystery. The eighth and last chapter is devoted to Mary. The placing is significant because many had wanted a separate decree on Mary, but in this chapter she is treated within the context of the church, as its model and archetype. The closest to a definition of the church comes in chapter 1:

> Christ, the one mediator, set up his holy church here on earth as a visible structure, a community of faith, hope and love; and he sustains it unceasingly and through it he pours out grace and truth on everyone. This society, however, equipped with hierarchical structures, and the mystical body of Christ, a visible assembly and a spiritual community, an earthly church and a church enriched with heavenly

gifts, must not be considered as two things, but as forming
one complex reality comprising a human and a divine ele-
ment. It is therefore by no mean analogy that it is likened
to the mystery of the incarnate Word. For just as the
assumed nature serves the divine Word as a living instrument of salvation inseparably joined with him, in a similar
way the social structure of the church serves the Spirit of
Christ who vivifies the church towards the growth of the
body [Ephesians 4:16]. . . .

This church, set up and organised in this world as a society, subsists in the catholic church, governed by the successor of Peter and the bishops in communion with him,
although outside its structures many elements of sanctification and of truth are to be found which, as proper gifts to
the church of Christ, impel towards catholic unity. [no. 8]

We see a shifting backward and forward between a more
hierarchical and institutional vision of the church and a more
mystical or mysterious one, illustrating well how the decrees of
Vatican II represent a patchwork quilt of different insights, a
many-colored garment. Particularly important is the last sentence quoted above in which it is said that the Church of Christ
"subsists in" (Latin, *subsistit in*) the Catholic Church. We know
from the various drafts of the decree that the phrase "subsists in"
represents a compromise, containing a certain elasticity of meaning. It is more comprehensive than "is," which would identify
the church of Christ exclusively with the Catholic Church—a
position advocated by some—yet the Catholic Church retains a
privileged position. The statement is clearly a development
beyond the earlier teaching, frequently and authoritatively
stated, that "there is no salvation outside the catholic church"
[D-H, nos. 870 and 875; above, pp. 56 and 73].

Regarding chapter 3 of the decree, "The Hierarchical Constitution of the Church and in Particular the Episcopate," a
"Preliminary Explanatory Note" (*Nota explicativa praevia*) was
issued, under pressure from the minority in the council who felt

that the chapter did not sufficiently safeguard the authority of the pope. The status of the note and its meaning are open to question. It was issued as a "clarification" of the doctrinal commission of the council and "at the command of higher authority," and was signed by Archbishop Felici, the secretary-general of the council. The "higher authority" was not specified, and though it may be taken as indicating the approval of Pope Paul VI the note was not promulgated in his name, and it was not formally approved by the council; in a sense its status hangs in the air. The note emphasizes that the collegiality of the bishops does not imply that the pope is a mere equal with his fellow bishops, that he retains an independent and superior authority. Many doubted whether the explanatory note added anything to the decree, and therefore whether it was necessary. A good result, however, was that the decree itself subsequently received the almost unanimous approval of the council.

The decree on the church, usually referred to as *Lumen gentium* from its opening words, was a cornerstone of the council. Many other decrees were developments or expansions of its individual chapters. Thus, those on the Eastern Catholic churches and on ecumenism, approved on the same day as *Lumen gentium*, concern two dimensions of the church: the eastern churches in communion with Rome and Christians not in communion with Rome.

The decree on ecumenism is particularly important and represents a major breakthrough. In view of the strong language of previous centuries against schism and heresy, it is not surprising that the decree was hotly debated, with many unwilling to break radically from the traditional language. In the end, however, the decree showed much generosity. It accepts that Catholics must take their share of blame for the divisions among Christians and that the living cannot be blamed for the sins of their ancestors. Other Christians are spoken of as "brothers and sisters," and the unity that already exists is emphasized; there is unity through Baptism and "some, even most, of the significant elements and endowments which together go to build up and give life to the church itself can exist outside the visible boundaries of the catholic church: the written word of God; the life of grace; faith, hope and charity, with the other interior gifts of the holy Spirit; and visible elements too" [no. 3]. The decree recognizes, however, that obstacles remain to full communion, and it urges Catholics to do their best to overcome them. It gives a privileged position to the Orthodox and other eastern communions, recognizing them as churches, while speaking more hesitantly of the "churches and ecclesial communities" resulting from the sixteenth-century Reformation in the West. Among the latter "the Anglican communion occupies a special place" [no. 13]—a position that was reinforced a few years later by the exceptionally warm welcome that Pope Paul VI accorded to the archbishop of Canterbury, Michael Ramsey, when they met in Rome and by the pope's subsequent reference to the Anglican church as the "ever beloved sister" of the Roman Catholic Church [*AAS*, vol. 62, 1970, p. 753].

All the remaining decrees received approval during the fourth and last year of the council.

The decree on the renewal of religious life exercised a huge influence on the subsequent reform of religious orders. It urged their members, men and women, to return to the original charism of the order and to adapt to the signs of the time: a twofold task that has proved challenging indeed! The problem was that religious orders had become too fossilized in many of their arrangements, in the manner of dress or in the observance of minute and restrictive rules, for example, so that when change was set in motion the result was more like a dam bursting than the orderly and organic development that the decree hoped for.

Dei verbum, on revelation, is the most theological decree. It had in mind Trent's decree on Scripture and tradition and sought to link them together more closely. "Hence sacred tradition and scripture are bound together in a close and reciprocal relationship. They flow from the same divine wellspring, merge together to some extent, and are on course towards the same end. . . . Tradition and scripture together form a single sacred deposit of the word of God, entrusted to the church." It also emphasizes the person or event of Christ as the source of revelation, rather than Trent's more intellectual and propositional "gospel," which Christ "first proclaimed with his own lips" [nos. 4, 7, and 9; above, p. 79].

The decree accepted, too, many of the principles of biblical criticism. Attention must be paid to the human dimension in the composition of the Bible as well as to the inspiration of the Holy Spirit. "God chose and employed human agents, using their own powers and faculties, in such a way that they wrote as authors in the true sense, and yet God acted in and through them." And therefore, "In order to get at what the biblical writers intended, attention should be paid . . . to literary *genres*" [nos. 11–12]. This was a major change from the uncritical approach that had been prevalent in much Catholic teaching during the Modernist crisis of the earlier part of the century, and it gave official blessing to the work of Catholic biblical scholars. Also, inasmuch as biblical criticism owed its inspiration primarily to Protestant scholars, it was another example of how Vatican II implicitly acknowledged the contributions made by the churches of the Reformation.

Two decrees looked to the world beyond Christianity: *Nostra aetate* on non-Christian religions and *Dignitatis humanae* on religious freedom. The former is brief and very cautious. "The catholic church rejects nothing of those things which are true and holy in these religions. It regards with respect those ways of acting and living and those precepts and teachings which, though often at variance with what it holds and expounds, frequently reflect a ray of that truth which enlightens everyone" [no. 2]. At least the council addressed itself to, and said something positive about, the great world religions of Hinduism, Buddhism, Islam, and Judaism. It was not ready to say anything fuller with any unanimity, yet it has proved influential in the Roman Catholic Church's subsequent relations with these and other religions.

> In Hinduism the divine mystery is explored and propounded with an inexhaustible wealth of myths and penetrating philosophical investigations, and liberation is sought from the distresses of our state either through various forms of ascetical life or deep meditation or taking refuge in God with loving confidence. In Buddhism, according to its various forms, the radical inadequacy of this changeable world is acknowledged and a way is taught whereby those with a devout and trustful spirit may be able to reach either a state of perfect freedom or, relying on their own efforts or on help from a higher source, the highest illumination. . . . The church looks on Muslims with respect. They worship the one God living and subsistent, merciful and almighty, creator of heaven and earth, who has spoken to humanity and to whose decrees, even the hidden ones, they seek to submit themselves wholeheartedly. . . . The church acknowledges that through the people with whom God out of his ineffable mercy deigned to enter into an ancient covenant, it received the revelation of the Old Testament and is nourished from the root of the good olive tree, onto which the branches of the wild olive tree of the gentiles have been grafted. [nos. 2–4]

The decree on religious freedom was stronger and fuller. It was hotly debated because many bishops, especially from the traditionally Catholic countries, wanted to preserve the ideal of a Christian state and because the proposed decree seemed hard to reconcile with previous condemnations of religious freedom, notably by Pope Pius IX in his Syllabus of Errors in 1864 [D-H, nos. 2915 and 2977–79]. It implied change in the church's teaching, more than just development. In the end, however, the decree was passed, recognizing a legitimate pluralism within society and the rights of all citizens. Much of the initiative came from the bishops of the United States of America, where Catholics wanted to live harmoniously in a pluralist society; especially influential was the American Jesuit John Courtney Murray, who attended the council as a *peritus* (expert) and was largely responsible for drafting the decree.

The last decree to be approved was *Gaudium et spes*, on the church in the world of today. This long decree may be seen as both a summary of the council's work and an application to life in the church and outside it. It is the first decree in the history of ecumenical and general councils to be addressed directly to the wider world. "The second Vatican council now immediately addresses itself not just to the church's own sons and daughters and all who call on the name of Christ but to people everywhere . . ." [no. 2]. The headings of the chapters, given above, provide some flavor of the document. It is direct, entering into the details of this life and its difficulties as well as our aspirations for eternal life. Certainly its starting point is positive toward the whole human endeavor; some would say it is naively optimistic; but this is not really fair, and there are no illusions about the damaging effects of sin. The opening sentence sets the tone: "The joys and hopes and the sorrows and anxieties of people today, especially of those who are poor and afflicted, are also the joys and hopes, sorrows and anxieties of the disciples of Christ, and there is nothing truly human which does not also affect them" [no. 1]. On one issue the council chose, perhaps unwisely, not to express its mind: contraception and other methods of birth control. The matter was left to a papal commission and resulted a few years later in the encyclical *Humanae vitae*, which caused massive divisions within the Catholic community. In general, however, the decree may be seen as leading the council out into the realities of life.

The sixteen decrees were eventually approved by large

majorities, certainly sufficient to fulfill the principle of "virtual unanimity," despite the vigorous debates that had gone into their making. There is a grading in the status of the decrees, though the distinctions were never defined officially. Three were called "declarations": those on education, non-Christian religions, and religious freedom. This is the lowest status, probably accorded in at least the second and third cases because there was not sufficient unanimity for a fuller or more authoritative statement. Nine were styled "decrees," and four given the more solemn title of "constitution." Of the latter, that on the liturgy has no further qualification; those on the church and revelation are "dogmatic" constitutions; that on the church in the world of today is a "pastoral" constitution. Those who prefer the constitution on the church tend to say that "dogmatic" gives an added authority, while those who prefer the constitution on the church in the world of today argue that "pastoral" and "dogmatic" imply only a difference of subject matter, not of authority. Indeed they may argue that the latter, as the last decree and a summary of the council's work, has the greater status. The sixteen decrees were in the form of essays and exhortations rather than dogmatic definitions or disciplinary canons, and none of them contained anathemas, in both of which respects the decrees differed from those of most previous councils.

Some 2,300 persons attended as members of the council at any given time (about 2,800 altogether, but some died during the four years and were replaced by others). The large majority were bishops, representing almost all the Roman Catholic sees in the world; some heads of religious orders and other officials also attended as members. Most bishops brought one or two theologians to assist them, and these *periti* (experts) had a certain official status and participated in drafting the decrees, though without being voting members of the council. Some *periti* appear to have been specially influential: Monsignor G. Philips from Belgium; E. Schillebeeckx, O.P., from the Netherlands; Hans Küng from Switzerland and Germany; Bernard Häring, C.S.Sp., and Karl Rahner, S.J., from Germany; Yves Congar, O.P., Henri de Lubac, S.J., and Jean Daniélou, S.J., from France; John Courtney Murray from the United States. In addition, churches of the Orthodox and Protestant traditions, and others, were invited to send observers, and they too made a contribution, notably to the decree on ecumenism.

In terms of numbers and representation worldwide, therefore, Vatican II was the largest and most ecumenical council in the history of the church, even though it was a council only of the Roman Catholic Church. The equilibrium, however, was less balanced than the worldwide representation suggests. The principal initiative in rejecting the draft decrees of the preparatory commission and in composing the decrees that were eventually approved came from a relatively small group of prelates and theologians mostly from northwestern Europe: Bernard Alfrink, Leo Joseph Suenens, Achilles Liénart, Joseph Frings, Julius Döpfner, Franz König, and Giacomo Lercaro, respectively cardinal archbishops of Utrecht, Mechlin-Brussels, Lille, Cologne, Munich-Freising, Vienna, and Bologna; the German Jesuit Cardinal Bea; and the *periti* mentioned earlier. To many, indeed, the whole council appeared European in its concerns and outlook: somewhat naive in its optimism and reflecting the relative prosperity of western Europe in the 1950s and early 1960s. Reception of the council's decrees, as a result, has been generally less engaged outside the western world than inside it. Christians of Latin American, Asia, and Africa, central and eastern Europe, have not felt the same affinity with the council. Their interests and concerns were not addressed so directly: for example, oppression and structural injustice, for which the western world bears much responsibility, popular religion of a nonwestern kind, and so on. Nevertheless this distance should not be exaggerated.

Even if these churches outside Europe subsequently pursued paths of their own, the new directions may well have become possible only because of the changes initiated by the council.

Within the western world reactions to the council were both more engaged and more polarized. In the immediate aftermath there was much enthusiasm, but problems emerged as the decrees came to be implemented, for example, regarding the liturgy and the reform of religious orders. Another issue has been the interpretation of the decrees. They contain many strands, and there is the temptation to quote from them selectively to support a particular agenda rather than to see them in the round. The council, moreover, cannot be limited to its decrees; it was an event that must be seen in terms of the people involved and above all of the Holy Spirit's guidance of the church. The tensions arising from the council should not be exaggerated, especially in comparison with the reception of various other councils. Only the relatively small group of followers of Archbishop Lefebvre have rejected the council outright and gone into schism, though others have adopted a minimalist or negative approach toward the council. For most it has been more a matter of digesting and gradually coming to terms with a truly momentous event in the life of the church.

Reaction from outside the Roman Catholic communion, moreover, has been generally favorable, especially from the Protestant churches, at least as a step in the right direction. There were fervent hopes for corporate reunion with some churches, notably the Anglican communion, but recently the movement has slowed, with obstacles arising on both sides. Even so, Vatican II has proved a huge step forward in ecumenical relations and has changed the agenda for reunion radically.

More than thirty years after the end of the council, it is still too early to come to a proper appreciation of its fruits, though some major assessments have been attempted recently [2e:

Latourelle, 1988–89; Alberigo, 1995–]. There is nothing surprising in this. It took at least a century to digest Trent and some other major councils. Surely the most important event in the life of the church in the twentieth century, the effects of Vatican II in the twenty-first century remain to be seen.

Conclusion and the Future

We have come to the end of a long story—at least until the next ecumenical council takes place! It is a very remarkable story, and that is perhaps the first and most important thing to remember. It forms a great wonder of the Christian community and later of the Roman Catholic Church more particularly, the most remarkable series of meetings in the history of the world.

The achievement can be seen in different ways. The theologian and the Christian believer can ponder the action of the Holy Spirit in guiding the church through the centuries. After the Bible, the twenty-one ecumenical and general councils form the single most important source of teaching in the church. Together they have something profound and authoritative to say on almost every aspect of Christian belief and practice. Somehow the Holy Spirit has preserved the church through these councils and many other local ones, enabling Christians to remain in contact with their roots and at the same time to grow, develop, and adapt through history: to keep Christianity a living and vital force. It is an astonishing achievement when one considers the sinful human beings involved and the exalted nature of the mystery to be communicated.

At the human level, too, the councils capture our imagination. First, in terms of antiquity. In comparison with the Althing of Iceland or the Parliament of Britain, for example, probably the oldest national assemblies with an institutional continuity in the western world, the councils of the Christian church yield a much longer history: the first Althing dates around 930 and the earliest Parliament is usually dated to 1257; the First Council of

114

Nicaea was held in 325. In terms of the gatherings of other world religions, it is hard to find a parallel.

The councils restore faith in the capacity of human nature. The participants confronted great issues of their day and the supreme challenge—so much more difficult—of presenting the mystery of Christ to the people of their time. They faced them with courage and directness and generally produced remarkably well-thought-out statements in response. They also achieved consensus, for the most part, so that the church (or the western church and the Roman Catholic Church later) was able to move ahead united. It is noticeable that the two most serious schisms in the church's history—between the eastern and western churches in the eleventh century and that resulting from the Reformation in the sixteenth century—occurred in the absence of councils, not as a result of them. Indeed they might well have been averted if a council had been called earlier. The councils represent one of the great collective achievements of humankind.

All this can be said without being starry-eyed. Frailty and sin are only too obvious: politicking, both secular and ecclesiastical, stubbornness, fierce language about opponents, inadequate and flawed responses. Much of the fascination of the councils is the interplay of so many levels of human response, reflecting the wider interaction of the human and the divine.

It is very important for Christians to appreciate this remarkable chapter in their history. Unfortunately the conciliar tradition has fallen under something of a cloud for Roman Catholics, largely as a result of the struggle between council and pope in the fifteenth century. The whole tradition has been compromised in the eyes of some Catholics, seen as a rival and a threat especially to papal teaching, and as a result it has been marginalized. This is foolish and quite unnecessary, especially since in principle there should be no clash between the two institutions, rather mutual corroboration. For other churches, more-

over, the medieval and later general councils are seen as irre-
deemably Roman Catholic and therefore are largely rejected. As
a result, with a truncated conciliar history interrupted after the
Second Council of Nicaea in 787, there is not among these
churches the interest in a living and continuous conciliar tradition that there might be. This too is a pity and might be at least
partly resolved by the more ecumenical and relaxed approach to
the councils after Nicaea II that has been suggested [above, pp.
50–51 and 75–76].

Interest in the councils is forward looking. They are not
just museum pieces of concern only to the historian. We have
already seen how the best councils were able to foresee the needs
of the future, as well as to speak to their own age. Certainly this
seems true of Vatican II, which continues to be quoted so much.
The conciliar process, moreover, which Vatican II did much to
encourage, seems vital for the future of the church.

The process is crucial for ecumenical relations between the
churches. Conciliar government is central to the Orthodox and
other churches of the East, and it was accepted in various forms
by almost all the churches of the Reformation. In any form of
church order that is to be acceptable to these churches, therefore, councils will have to find an integral place. Also, the teachings of the early councils form a common heritage for the
Christian community. Thus, we are often reminded how the
Christian churches are united in Baptism, by acceptance of the
Bible, by good works, and so on; but we are also united by our
acceptance of the early councils, before the disastrous split
between the East and West in the eleventh century: an acceptance that is both a guarantee of existing unity and a point of reference for future endeavors toward more perfect communion.
Finally, a proper recognition of the later councils, including their
more limited status as general councils of the western church
and later of the Roman Catholic Church, forms a key to ecumenical progress, as has been argued; it helps to prevent Trent

and Vatican I being given an absolute status and therefore becoming a block to ecumenical dialogue.

"Sobornost," derived from the Russian *sobiratj*, "to gather" or "a state of being united," and from the similar Slavonic word *soborny*, developed as a theological concept, especially by the Russian theologians Alexis Khomiakov (1804–1860) and Sergius Bulgakov (1871–1944), to denote the unity of many persons within the organic fellowship of the church—a blend of catholicity, integrality, communality, conciliarity, collegiality, and collectivity. "Sobornost," patterned on the communal unity of the first Christians and roughly corresponding to the Greek κοινωνία, may be a way forward. It is seen as contrasting with the exaggerated emphasis on juridical authority in the Roman Catholic Church and the excessive individualism of the churches of the Reformation. Indeed, all three main Christian traditions—Orthodox, Roman Catholic, and Reformed—can learn much from each other. Thus, the Orthodox churches, despite their advocacy of conciliarity and collegiality, have in practice had considerable difficulty in holding effective synods. The Roman Catholic Church, despite a tradition of at times almost monarchical authority and unease with councils, has, paradoxically, held a number of exceptionally effective general councils from the Middle Ages onwards; and many Reformed churches have managed to combine emphasis upon individual salvation with a form of regular synodal government.

Within the Roman Catholic communion, too, greater attention to conciliarity, in its various forms, seems vital to the health of the church. Pope Paul VI said on several occasions that the papacy is the greatest obstacle to reunion, and Pope John Paul II's recent encyclical *Ut unum sint* invited Christians to suggest ways for the papacy to become more acceptable and effective. A more conciliar papacy may be an apposite suggestion: both council and pope would be strengthened, not weakened, by fuller collaboration. Indeed, the point was partly recognized by Paul VI when in 1965 he established the "synod of bishops" as a permanent body charged with advising him on matters of importance to the whole church. The assemblies (or synods) have been held every two or three years since then [see above, p. 2].

The early councils especially show how inventive the church can be regarding the arrangements of councils. We have seen how the languages, locations, procedures, and participants of the councils have varied in the course of time. While the present requirements of canon law should be observed, of course, the variety of regulations in the past shows how much flexibility is possible in the future. For example, as women were admitted to several early councils, so there seems no reason in principle why they could not be admitted again; at Vatican II some women were admitted as "auditors." Many, almost endless, possibilities are opened up under the inspiration of the Holy Spirit.

Indeed, especially the early councils suggest that the church today could adapt itself much more to the forms of secular society. It is often said that the church has its own structures, which are not those of the secular world. This is true, but the distinction should not be exaggerated. The early councils saw the church adapting itself to a large extent to the existing forms of secular government, except where this proved incompatible with the gospel. Today, too, the church need not set itself apart from modern society more than is necessary. It can learn much from the latter, and indeed it has a golden opportunity to take a lead. The early councils led their age in democracy and in other forms of government; the church could do the same today rather than lag behind!

This book is a brief guide to the highest peaks of a brilliant mountain range. But often the foothills and the way up are as interesting as the peaks, so you may now wish to go to the texts themselves. The full decrees of the twenty-one ecumenical and general councils are available in translation in English, French, and Italian; they soon will be in German and Malayalam, as well as in their Greek and Latin originals [above, pp. 10–11]. No secondary work can substitute for the texts. As well as fascinating reading, they provide a fuller context for what has been said in this book. After that there is the rest of "Mansi," for more leisurely reading!

Bibliography

This select bibliography contains (1) the most important works on the councils (2) other works cited in this book. Those listed in the Abbreviations (above, p. vii) are not mentioned again here.

1. General Works

Primary Sources

The main editions of the councils are reviewed on pp. 7–11 above.

Secondary Works

Alberigo, G., ed. *Storia dei Concili Ecumenici.* Brescia: Queriniana, 1990.

Bermejo, L. M. *Church, Conciliarity and Communion.* Anand: Gujavar Sahitya Prakash, 1990.

Brandmüller, W., general editor. *Konziliengeschichte*, 24 vols. so far. Paderborn: Schöningh, 1979–. Series A = Darstellungen (monographs on individual councils), series B = Untersuchungen (especially important are the volumes by H. J. Sieben on conciliar theory from the early church to the twentieth century).

Congar, Y. "Structures ecclésiales et conciles dans les relations entre Orient et Occident." *Revue des sciences philosophiques et théologiques* 58 (1974): 355–90.

Davis, L. D. *The First Seven Ecumenical Councils.* Wilmington: Glazier, 1987.

Dumeige, G., general editor. *Histoire des Conciles Oecuméniques*, 12 vols. so far. Paris: Éditions de l'Orante, 1963–.

Dvornik, F. *The Ecumenical Councils*. New York: Hawthorn Books, 1961.

Hefele, H. J., and H. Leclerq. *Histoire des Conciles,* 11 vols. Paris: Letouzey et Ané, 1907–52.

Helmrath, J. "Konziliensammlungen." *Lexikon für Theologie und Kirche*, 3d ed. Freiburg im Breisgau: Herder, 1993–. Vol. 6, cols. 351–55.

Hughes, P. E. *The Church in Crisis: A History of the General Councils*. New York: Image Books, 1964.

Jedin, H., general editor. *History of the Church*, 10 vols. London: Burns & Oates, 1980 (= English translation of *Handbuch der Kirchengeschichte*. Freiburg: Herder, 1965).

Jedin, H. *Ecumenical Councils in the Catholic Church*. London: Nelson, 1960 (= English translation of *Kleine Konziliengeschichte*. Freiburg: Herder, 1959).

Murphy, J. L. *The General Councils of the Church*. Milwaukee: Bruce, 1960.

Oakley, F. *Council over Pope?* New York: Herder and Herder, 1969.

Percival, H. R., ed. *The Seven Ecumenical Councils of the Undivided Church*, Nicene and Post-Nicene Fathers, vol. 14. 1900.

Peri, V. "Il numero dei concili ecumenici nella tradizione cattolica moderna." *Aevum* 37 (1963): 433–501.

Schatz, K. *Allgemeine Konzilien: Brennpunkte der Kirchengeschichte*. Paderborn: Schöningh, 1997.

Sesboüé, B. general editor. *Histoire des Dogmes*, 4 vols. Paris: Desclée, 1994–96.

Sieben, H. J. See Brandmüller above.

Watkin, E. I. *The Church in Council*. London: Darton, Longman and Todd, 1960.

Useful articles and bibliographies on individual councils are to be found in various dictionaries and encyclopedias: *Enciclopedia cattolica* (Vatican City: Ente per l'Enciclopedia cattolica e per il Libro cattolica, 1949–54); *Dictionnaire de théologie catholique* (Paris: Letouzey et Ané, 1903–50); *Lexikon für Theologie und Kirche* (2d ed., Freiburg im Breisgau: Herder, 1957–68; 3d ed., 10 vols. so far, Freiburg im Breisgau: Herder, 1993–); *New Catholic Encyclopedia* (New York, 1967); *Oxford Dictionary of the Christian Church*, ed. F. L. Cross and E. A. Livingstone (3d ed.,

Oxford: Oxford University Press, 1997); J. N. D. Kelly, *The Oxford Dictionary of Popes* (Oxford: Oxford University Press, 1986).

Introductions to and fuller bibliographies for the twenty-one ecumenical and general councils are to be found in A-T (Abbreviations, above p. vii).

2. Particular Councils

(a) Early Councils

Chadwick, H. "The Origin of the Title 'Oecumenical council.'" *Journal of Theological Studies* 23 (1972): 132–35.

Davis, L. D. *The First Seven Ecumenical Councils: Their History and Theology.* Collegeville: Liturgical Press, 1987.

Dossetti, G. L. *Il simbolo di Nicaea e di Costantinopoli.* Rome: Herder, 1967.

Festugière, A. J., ed. and trans. *Éphèse et Chalcédoine: Actes des conciles.* Paris: Beauchesne, 1982.

Grillmeier, A. *Christ in Christian Tradition.* London: Mowbrays, 1975– (= English version of *Jesus der Christus im Glauben der Kirche.* Freiburg: Herder, 1979–).

Hanson, R. P. *The Search for the Christian Doctrine of God: The Arian Controversy, 318–381.* Edinburgh: T. & T. Clark, 1988.

Kelly, J. N. D. *Early Christian Creeds.* 3d ed., London: Longman, 1972.

Nedungatt, G., and M. Featherstone, eds. *The Council in Trullo Revisited.* Rome: Pontificio Istituto Orientale, 1995.

Peri, V. "C'è un concilio oecumenico ottavo?" *Annuarium Historiae Conciliorum* 8 (1976): 52–79.

Tanner, N. P. "The African Contribution to the First Five Ecumenical Councils." *Afer (African Ecclesial Review)* 33 (1991): 201–13.

Young, F. *From Nicaea to Chalcedon.* London: SCM, 1983.

(b) Medieval Councils

Alberigo, G., ed. *Christian Unity: The Council of Ferrara-Florence 1438/39–1989.* Leuven: Leuven University Press, 1991.

Brandmüller, W. *Das Konzil von Konstanz*, 2 vols. Paderborn: Schöningh, 1991–97.

Crowder, C. M. D. *Unity, Heresy and Reform 1378–1460: The Conciliar Response to the Great Schism*. London: Edward Arnold, 1977.

Ferrer, Boniface. *Tractatus pro Defensione Benedicti XIII*, in vol. 2 of *Thesaurus Novus Anecdotum*, ed. E. Martène and U. Durand. Paris: F. Delaelne, 1717.

Figgis, J. N. *Studies in Political Thought from Gerson to Grotius, 1414–1625*. Cambridge: Cambridge University Press, 1907.

Garcia y Garcia, A., ed. *Constitutiones Concilii Quarti Lateranensis una cum Commentariis Glossatum*, Monumenta Iuris Canonici, series A, vol. 2. Vatican City: Libreria Editrice Vaticana, 1981.

Gill, J. *The Council of Florence*. Cambridge: Cambridge University Press, 1959.

Morris, C. *The Papal Monarchy 1050–1250*. Oxford: Clarendon, 1989.

Morrissey, T. "The Decree *Haec sancta* and Cardinal Zabarella." *Annuarium Historiae Conciliorum* 10 (1978): 145–78.

Sayers, J. *Innocent III: Leader of Europe 1198–1216*. London: Longman, 1994.

Pantin, W. *The English Church in the Fourteenth Century*. Cambridge: Cambridge University Press, 1955.

Tierney, B. *Foundations of the Conciliar Theory*. Cambridge: Cambridge University Press, 1955.

(c) Trent

Jedin, H. *A History of the Council of Trent*, 2 vols. only. London: Nelson, 1957–61 (= English translation of part of *Geschichte des Konzils von Trient*, 4 vols. in 5. Freiburg im Breisgau: Herder, 1951–75).

———. *Crisis and Closure of the Council of Trent*. London: Sheed & Ward, 1967 (= English translation of *Krisis und Abschluss des Trienter Konzils 1562/3*. Freiburg: Herder, 1964).

(d) Vatican I

Butler, C. *The Vatican Council 1869–70*, 2 vols. London: Longmans, Green and Co., 1932; London: Collins, 1962.

Hasler, A. B. *How the Pope Became Infallible*. New York: Doubleday, 1981 (= abbreviated English translation of *Pius IX (1846–1878): Päpstliche Unfehlbarkeit und 1. Vatikanisches Konzil*. Stuttgart: Hiersemann, 1977).

Hennesey, J. *The First Council of the Vatican: The American Experience*. New York: Herder and Herder, 1963.

Schatz, K. *Vaticanum I. 1869–1870*, 3 vols. Paderborn: Schöningh, 1992–94.

(e) Vatican II

Alberigo, G., and J. Komonchak, eds. *History of Vatican II*, 3 of 5 vols. so far. Maryknoll, N.Y.: Orbis; Leuven: Peeters, 1995–; appearing also in French, German, Italian, Portugese, and Spanish.

Latourelle, R., ed. *Vatican II: Assessment and Perspectives*, 3 vols. Mahwah: Paulist, 1988–89; also in French and Italian.

Stacpoole, A., ed. *Vatican II by Those Who Were There*. London: Geoffrey Chapman, 1986.

Vorgrimler, H., ed. *Commentary on the Documents of Vatican II*, 5 vols. London: Burns & Oates, 1967–79.

Appendix

List of Ecumenical and General Councils

Early Church	Middle Ages	Modern Era
Nicaea I (325)	Lateran I (1123)	Trent (1545–1563)
Constantinople I (381)	Lateran II (1139)	Vatican I (1869–1870)
Ephesus (431)	Lateran III (1179)	Vatican II (1962–1965)
Chalcedon (451)	Lateran IV (1215)	
Constantinople II (553)	Lyons I (1245)	
Constantinople III (680–681)	Lyons II (1274)	
Nicaea II (787)	Vienne (1311–1312)	
Constantinople IV (869–870)	Constance (1414–1418)	
	Basel-Florence (1431–1445)	
	Lateran V (1512–1517)	

Index